Out of Office

Brooke E. Rye

Out of Office

A Retirement Memoir of Stepping Back, Showing Up, and Sucking at New Things

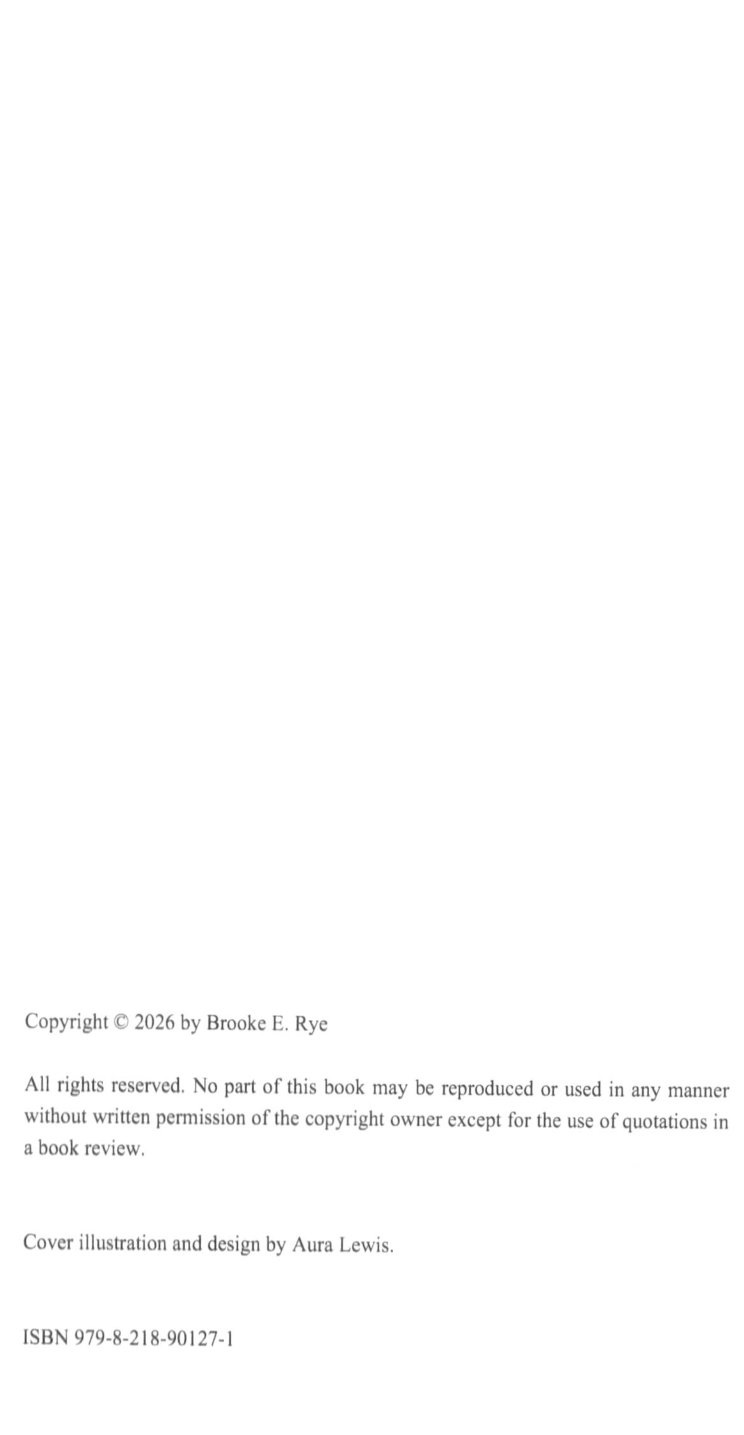

Dedication

For Dad, who taught me all the outdoor things, and for Scott, who helped me remember them.

Contents

Prologue

If you are not a cyclist, you might not be familiar with "clipping in," or attaching bike pedals to the cleats of the soles of specialized cycling shoes. This connection increases pedaling efficiency by converting effort into forward momentum while keeping the feet stable.

Most cyclists master clipping in early on as a rite of passage. I did not. For years, I rode with clip-ready shoes precariously balanced on clip-ready pedals, tackling sixty-five-mile rides and steep grades. I climbed to Jamestown and Ward, former mining towns in the foothills of Boulder. I joined organized rides in Colorado and New Mexico—the Buffalo Bicycle Classic Epic Gravel, the Winter Park Crooked Gravel, and the Santa Fe Gravelón. I climbed Switzerland Trial, Gold Hill, and Vail Pass. None of it clipped in.

When I have told fellow cyclists that I was not clipping in, their reactions were something like…

"What?! What the actual—How is that even possible? You *have* to clip in. How can you *not* clip in?"

I know they are right, but clipping in feels intimidating—complicated, confining, and risky. I have clipped in before, but only for stationary spin classes. On the trail or open road? Terrifying.

My husband Scott, a seasoned road cyclist, assures me, "Everybody falls. You'll fall. It's embarrassing, but you get back up. No big deal."

Embarrassing?! Please. At a stoplight on Sunset Boulevard, to the delight of my colleague sitting shotgun, I once rolled down my window to ask the driver of a Jaguar if he had any Grey Poupon, to which he replied, "Yeah, lady. I'm sittin' on a whole f*cking case of it!" I have sung karaoke—sober—in a packed sushi bar, performed a beer-balancing party trick—not sober—too far into my thirties, and belted out "Santa Baby" through a bullhorn during a boat parade. And I can't sing.

I could not give a jar of f*cks about being embarrassed! What I fear is being too attached to the bike, unable to separate myself from it, falling, and breaking bones.

Perhaps I experience a type of athletic anxiety. Not quite a phobia. Not social anxiety, where one worries about being judged in front of studio mirrors or farting during downward dog, but physical fear. A somatic dread. I feel this—as well as a sense of awe and humility—on the ski lift on the mountain, on a hiking trail that includes scrambling, scree, and exposure, and upon meeting up with my cycling group to ride an unfamiliar route into the foothills. Falling while downhill skiing is considered a feature, not a bug. High altitude hiking can include exposure—what my friends call "death on the left," routes that pose a risk of falling down steep terrain. And dying. Bombing down winding mountain roads frequented by deer and the occasional bear will take your breath away. Mountain sports hit different.

I recalled a hike that Scott and I did in Montana's Glacier National Park with waterfalls and wildflowers, a gorgeous trail that wound across streams and through forests, opening up to incredible views at the summit. We removed our packs and stood on the peak, taking pictures and searching for a reasonably flat spot on which to sit and eat homemade burritos. As I admired the blue glacier lake across the rocky chasm and jagged granite peaks, I was struck by the urge to lie flat and pin my body as close to the ground as possible, as though if I didn't, I would be sucked into the gorge.

My intense appreciation of the staggering beauty caused me to feel simultaneous wonder, dread, and the need to lie prone and face down in the dirt. It left me in...awe. The scale of the Rocky Mountains wilderness—its altitude, sunshine, and grandiose, unrelenting beauty—has the effect of eclipsing all previous encounters with nature, making them feel like a warm-up for the real thing. A lore surrounds the power of the mountains as we become keenly aware of altitude, its effects, and our own fragility. In summer, I have hustled to descend the mountain before noon to avoid thunderstorms. Hydration, then, was no longer a healthy "should" but a necessity. I layered high-tech fabrics to wick, breathe, and dry quickly because, as hikers say, "cotton kills." But "Feel the fear and do it anyway," right?

I know I cannot progress without taking the leap, so I cross the Rubicon and text Scott.

"I'd like to work on clipping in."

Everything online described clipping in as "a secure connection between your shoes and your pedals," so it is difficult to explain my irrational fear. Is there loss of control when it takes two movements—instead of one—to get my foot from the pedal to the ground? Is it attachment to a thing outside of myself? Or is the panic of being locked in when I want an exit, a half-second delay between falling and saving myself, stretching into something bigger?

One

This Leisure You Speak Of...

I did not always have hobbies, let alone passions. When I thought of passion, I thought of slow kisses and steamy sex, not…Pilates. In my past life as a software project manager super-commuting in Southern California, driving four hours to and from work daily, I had no time for hobbies or passions. Time not spent working or driving demanded meal preparation, errand running, and daily fitness classes to sustain my rigorous lifestyle. On weekends, I recovered from the week prior and prepared for the week ahead, Saturday mornings spent over coffee, mindlessly lazing on the sofa viewing Pinterest capsule wardrobes and tiny homes. I spent Scary Sundays grocery shopping, meal planning, and staving off internal darkness.

And then my husband Scott and I, along with our twelve-year-old yellow Labrador, Motu, moved to Singapore in 2015, where I would experience a brief stint as a trailing spouse. We met our realtor, Lewis, in the lobby of the beautiful Shangri-La hotel just prior to our tour that would exactly mirror HGTV's *House Hunters International*.

"Brooke, what are your leisure activities?" Lewis asked.

Actually, he asked me twice because the first time I did not answer. I could not answer and was laid bare. I was literally sitting in Shangri-La being asked what I wanted to do over the next two years.

Thankfully, today—ten years later—my answer to this question is vastly different!

My brief stint as a trailing spouse in Singapore ended after a year, mostly because I became ill. When we returned stateside, I could not imagine returning to a super-commute, though I knew I would return to project management at some point. Scott, weary from international travel and weeks at a time away from home, decided to retire from his career as a corporate pilot. Supported by savings, we took a mid-life version of (nearly) a gap year to heal and visited national parks, hiked, and camped. I was forty-five, and Scott was forty-eight—if averages were on our side, we were only halfway through our lives.

I thought about my childhood in the rural foothills of Northern California and the active, outdoorsy things our dad taught my sister and me—riding bikes, body surfing, playing tennis, alpine skiing, fishing, and building fires (campfires—we are not a family of arsonists). As an adult, I had allowed these pastimes to slip away, convinced that they took up too much time, that I needed to be more skilled, or that investing in them—whether time or money—would be wasted if I lost interest, my version of the sunk cost fallacy in reverse.

For years, I had been stuck in the belief that leisure must be optimized—that every rare hour of free time should be spent in the most productive way possible. If an activity did not burn calories, build skills, or create something tangible, it felt indulgent, wasteful even. In chasing efficiency, I had not given myself permission to fully enjoy my life. But that was about to change.

After Singapore, I began asking myself, "What would a fulfilling retirement look like?" One thing was certain: Whatever it was, it did not look like Southern California, and I remember the day Scott and I decided to leave.

It was December 2016, and we left our house in Long Beach at six in the morning, hoping to beat traffic and secure a parking spot at the trailhead. Our hike took us high above Malibu with sweeping views of the coastline. We shared a picnic lunch back at our car, then hit the road at two o'clock in the afternoon to drive home.

Sixty-six miles. Three and a half hours. On a Thursday.

After a perfect day of hiking on a clear, warm winter day, we were trapped in stop-and-go traffic, inching along Pacific Coast Highway at a glacial pace. The frustration built with every mile, our route oxblood red on the traffic app. We cussed—not at each other, but at the congestion, the sheer absurdity of it. We were in the wrong city, if not the wrong state, for hiking. The question bounced between us, "WTF are we still doing here? WTF is keeping us here?"

With nothing better to do while stuck in traffic, we started making plans to leave California. The proliferation of remote jobs and tech hubs around the country meant that we were no longer confined to a major coastal city—I could find work as a software project manager in another state. Scott wanted to learn more about the real estate market. We talked about selling our Long Beach home, downsizing, and purchasing an apartment building in Colorado for Scott to manage—a prohibitively expensive proposition in Southern California. We would drive to Denver, visit our friends, meet their real estate agent, and look at houses. If we could handle Colorado in January—one of its coldest, bleakest months—we could handle the other eleven. Our friends reassured us, "There is no such thing as bad weather, only bad clothes."

For us, a fulfilling retirement looked like Colorado. It looked like mountains and open space. Scott wanted to fly fish. I wanted to try cycling, something more than riding my beach cruiser on the strand. Camping, cycling, hiking, and skiing—everything outdoors would be at the heart of our next chapter. Retirement looked like deepening our connections: spending more time with my parents, my sister, and her family, and Scott's extended family. It looked like building new friendships in a locale that better suited us and aligned with our interests.

And it looked like getting up close and personal with my IRA. I reached out to my financial advisor, and we began discussing my retirement horizon—at least ten years out—and created a plan to meet regularly to review my investments. Neither Scott nor I were entitled to pensions or medical benefits—we had IRAs to provide for us in retirement.

And dogs. In retirement, there would be dogs.

Two

IRA

In Sanskrit, Ira is a female name that means "the earth," mother of all vegetation. In Hebrew, one of its many meanings is "watchful," and in Polynesian mythology Ira is the sky goddess and mother of the stars. The Internal Revenue Service is slightly less romantic, where IRA is an acronym for Individual Retirement Account.

I retired just days before my fifty-third birthday, closing the chapter on a working life that began at sixteen—eleven if you count babysitting and watering neighbors' yards. (If retiring at fifty-three sounds impossible and unrelatable, my forty-five-year-old self—the one without hobbies—felt the same.) My first payroll job was at an ice cream parlor. And with my first paycheck, I opened a savings account, received an ATM card, and committed to saving my earnings for college living expenses…at $3.25 an hour.

Throughout college and after graduation, I worked in retail. The mid-'90s were not exactly booming with technology jobs for liberal arts graduates, especially those with lackluster GPAs. And without social networking sites, even if jobs existed, they were difficult to find. I cycled through careers in my twenties, renting cars to Hollywood tourists, luxury car owners, and the occasional celebrity. Before smartphones and tablets, I waited for customers with my blank rental contracts and green clipboard, people-watched to pass the time in the lobbies of the Chateau

Marmont, the Church of Scientology's Château Élysée, and the lounges of Jaguar and Mercedes dealerships.

Though I was not particularly skilled at managing my finances in my early twenties, one decision changed my financial trajectory. At twenty-five, I landed my first "big girl" job selling copiers at Eastman Kodak, then a blue-chip company. The job came with a company car, a corporate American Express, and a 401(k) match. A colleague advised me to take full advantage of it, so from my first paycheck, I contributed the maximum via biweekly payroll deductions—15 percent of my pretax salary—to my 401(k). As they say, pay yourself first. That choice, along with a few other key decisions, had the greatest impact on my ability to leave my career at fifty-three.

I left Eastman Kodak to work for the financial services company Morgan Stanley, a brief stint as a stockbroker in downtown Los Angeles at the turn of the millennium, amid Y2K hype and Boom-Boom Room–era sexism. I rolled my 401(k) funds from Eastman Kodak into my newly opened IRA at Morgan Stanley. With those proceeds, I bought my first stocks—ten shares each of three stocks recommended by Philip Purcell during a speech he gave to broker trainees at the pre-9/11 World Trade Center in New York City. Those stocks were EchoStar, Kohls, and Eli Lilly. Words of wisdom I learned from my training were "It's not timing the market; it's time in the market."

With each subsequent employer over the next twenty-five years, I continued to contribute 15 percent of my pretax income to 401(k)s, purchasing mostly S&P 500 mutual funds (plus some small-cap funds) within employee-sponsored retirement plans. Each time I separated from an employer (hello, tech layoffs!), I rolled the 401(k) proceeds into my IRA and purchased growth and technology stocks based upon suggestions from my financial advisor—and then I held those stocks like a good girl. Buy and hold. Rinse and repeat.

The principle instilled in me during training was that long-term investors who stay the course through downturns typically benefit from the market's eventual recovery and growth. Market volatility did not concern me because my investment horizon was a matter of decades, and I did not sell my growth and technology stocks during the aughties Great Recession. This disciplined approach—along with low-cost index funds, dollar-cost averaging, and the power of compounding—is the unsexy reality of long-term investing.

Though diligent investing primarily enabled me to retire at fifty-three, other strategic choices also played a significant role. I met Scott just after starting at Eastman Kodak, and we purchased a small house in Long Beach around the turn of the millennium. We sold that house three years later to purchase a larger house and then refinanced in the aughties when borrowing money was inexpensive. We made intentional financial choices. We lived within our means, purchased pre-owned vehicles, and spent $1,000 on our wedding, including my dress. We remained child-free—DINKs (Dual Income, No Kids).

According to the Department of Agriculture, raising a child to the age of eighteen in our demographic would likely have cost about $280,000, or $15,555 per year, though costs are rarely linear. That figure represents only the basics, excluding higher education and additional costs like club sports, international travel, family vacations, lessons, tutors, prep courses, and uninsured medical treatments or therapies. Nor does it include organic blueberries.

From real estate decisions to lifestyle, our deliberate financial choices, factors that compounded over time, shaped our financial foundation. We made sound choices, but we also operated within systems that quietly but consistently worked in our favor, from stable housing markets to access to investment advice. I carry a deep sense of gratitude for my opportunities, knowing that many of the conditions that allowed me to step away from work early are not available to everyone.

And then life experiences in our forties and fifties altered our perspective on what truly mattered, and how much was enough. My father-in-law died in a tragic accident in 2007. My mother-in-law passed away from a rare blood cancer in 2014. I became seriously ill while living in Singapore in 2015. My mother was revived from cardiac arrest and saved by life-changing heart surgery in 2020. Illnesses and the passing of loved ones shifted our mindset, reminding us that financial security meant little if we spent our healthiest years working instead of living. Life felt fragile and ephemeral—entirely too valuable to be spent on someone else's schedule. I longed to spend more time doing things I could not do while working: taking painting classes, resuming a hot yoga practice, and traveling. I wanted to be with Scott, pulling into deserted campsites on Sunday afternoons and skiing empty slopes on Tuesday mornings. We began to ask ourselves, "How much is enough?"

Though working in the financial sector was just a brief stop on my winding career path to managing software projects, it gave me a solid foundation in portfolio basics and fee structures. I became familiar with different investment vehicles and the roles of financial professionals—Certified Financial Planners (CFPs), Financial Advisors, and brokers—and their compensation.

For decades, I had no issue paying commissions to purchase stocks in my IRA. My advisor conducted research I had no interest in doing, and her firm's recommendations helped my portfolio grow. I embraced a "set it and forget it" mentality, trusting that if I contributed regularly and invested in solid stocks, everything would work out. And it did. But that approach worked throughout my twenties, thirties, and forties. In my early fifties, I knew what had gotten me here would not carry me forward.

My IRA was packed with growth stocks—some highly volatile—and I had no clear strategy for shifting toward more stable investments. I had watched one of my stocks soar to the low 400s in late 2021, then plummet two years later, only to begin climbing again. I had never attempted to time the market and sell stocks at their historical highs—what if they kept rising? Only hindsight reveals the peaks and valleys of the market. Still, I needed to rebalance my portfolio and transition from growth stocks to income-generating assets with recurring cash flow. The challenge? I did not want to pay commissions to sell my existing positions and then also pay fees associated with managed income funds.

Retirement had always been a far-off goal, until it was not. By the time the pandemic subsided in 2021, my IRA had reached a number that made early distributions a viable option to replace earned income from my job. It was no longer a distant goal a decade away—I was looking at two to five years. But I did not have the luxury of waiting out another Great Recession. I had lived through its uncertainty from 2007 to 2009, watching portfolios shrink overnight, and I could not ignore that possibility. History may not repeat itself, but it often rhymes, and I was preparing to step away from a steady income. I felt paralyzed by the thought of a market downturn wiping out half my portfolio's value.

When I asked friends how they transitioned their portfolios, their responses were always the same. "Our financial planner figures that out." While I had no interest in managing my portfolio on a daily basis, handing over full control to a financial planner felt too passive and too expensive, as did handing over the bulk of my portfolio to a fee-based managed fund. I felt lost. The same financial planning industry that helped me grow a portfolio over three decades while I was working seemed bereft of options now that I needed to preserve assets and replace my income.

I had always been a person comfortable with structure and rules, and financial rules for retirement were no exception. Over the decades as I contributed to my IRA, I clung to rules. Rules made me feel safe, as though I was doing what I should be, and it seemed logical to follow at least some of them. The 10–15 percent savings rule says that 15 percent of one's gross income is a good amount to invest for retirement. The 80 percent rule suggests that, to maintain lifestyle, retirees should aim for 80 percent of their pre-retirement income. The rule of 25 estimates how much to save for retirement by estimating annual income required in retirement and then multiplying that number by 25. All solid rules. So, where were the rules to help me transition from an aggressive growth portfolio to a stable income portfolio?

Scott self-managed his IRA. After leaving aviation, he delved into real estate and learned about the markets and retirement investing as though it were a second career. He immersed himself in all things financial: books, blogs, magazines, podcasts, and webinars. Scott encouraged me to develop a plan—he texted me articles about ETFs (exchange-traded funds), sent me links to books and blog posts on retirement, and the IRS website for information on early IRA distributions. He provided tools, but I still felt stuck. And I felt silly for feeling stuck. During my tenure as a stockbroker, I had learned the fundamentals of stocks, bonds, mutual funds, and money markets, so why didn't I know what to do?

I also dreaded the conversation with my financial advisor of twenty years, whom I adored and admired. But her firm's model no longer aligned with my needs, and though I felt guilty about leaving, I knew it was the right decision. Nearly two years before retiring, I transferred my portfolio to a firm that offered greater flexibility. My advisor was as gracious as ever, wishing me well.

Gradually, over the next two years, I took steps toward diversification. I created a timeline to divest technology stocks, reducing risk—and night terrors—by ensuring they comprised a smaller portion of my portfolio. To better understand our responsibilities and tax liabilities during retirement, I read, re-read, and highlighted relevant sections of the IRS tax code associated with early IRA distributions while we worked with an early distribution specialist.

If Ira in Sanskrit means "the earth" and mother of all vegetation, maybe for me, IRA could also mean the mother of abundance.

I allocated a portion of my IRA to a managed fund focused on asset preservation and income generation. I added additional dividend-paying stocks to my portfolio and purchased ETFs and fixed-income vehicles to begin building an income stream. With each step, I felt a growing sense of stability—replacing fear with strategy and uncertainty with a plan. Scott and I began meeting regularly with our advisors, refining our retirement and distribution strategies. By developing a structured plan, I no longer felt paralyzed. I transformed my avoidance and anxiety into clarity and decisive action. If I awoke at two o'clock to use the bathroom, I no longer lay in bed thinking about technology stocks but instead replayed awkward conversations from five years ago like a normal person.

Three

Doomscrolling and Day Drinking

For years, Scott had been reading book excerpts and texting me articles about retirees—their changing lives, the unexpected emotional toll, and the readjustments they faced.

"You don't know how you'll feel once you give it up," he warned, speaking of my career.

Most retirement books focus on finances, resources for saving and investing. But I was uninterested in the retirement books my husband read, certain they would bore me. The books that were not about money did not appeal to me either—impersonal, written mostly by men, prescribing what I should be doing, feeling, or becoming.

I heard plenty of stories. Men so restless in retirement that they drifted back into lesser versions of their old careers, some as volunteers, others in part-time roles. Some took jobs at Home Depot. Some played golf obsessively. Some…just died. Both retired men and women, especially during the pandemic, spent their days glued to their tablets or televisions, swallowed by an endless cycle of news, waiting for cocktail hour. According to *US News*, retirees spend over four hours per day watching television—mostly the news. Doomscrolling and day drinking were two habits I had no desire to pick up.

I get it—leaving a career is an identity shift. But as I read these articles I started to wonder, *Were they mostly written by men, for men, about men? Why should I believe that women's emotional well-being in retirement was ever seriously considered?* The workplace is inherently sexist. Men hold more positions of status, earn higher salaries, and shape work cultures that reinforce their dominance. Hello, freezing-cold offices!

Women remain the second sex. We are excluded from medical studies, such as the Physicians' Health Study that led to the daily aspirin recommendation. Women are overlooked in the design of personal protective equipment (PPE), leaving us more vulnerable to harmful substances and infections. Female serial killers are less likely to be recognized because the definition of a serial killer has been shaped by male-centric biases. Even murder is not a motivating factor to include women! If not for Charlize Theron's gritty portrayal in *Monster*, would we know the name Aileen Wuornos? (Her middle name is Carol, by the way.)

Though I cannot solve the invisibility of women in a memoir—at least not this one—I wondered if retirement was sexist as well. And if so, could that benefit women? Since fewer of us reached high-status roles, maybe we would not struggle with their loss. If our strengths were undervalued in male-dominated workplaces, perhaps we would not miss being there. Maybe the competitive structures sidelining us would fade in importance, replaced by something better. If women spent years compartmentalized—in careers, managing households, and raising children—was retirement our opportunity to step outside those constraints? If we chose or remained in careers based on financial practicality, geography, or the needs of family and partners, perhaps retirement was our time to be who we wanted.

I began to wonder if retirement—instead of stripping away identity—could offer women the chance to step into something greater. The very skills we honed—collaboration, adaptability, emotional intelligence, and wisdom—might finally be valued in ways the workplace never allowed. Whether through volunteering, activism, or organizing events, perhaps we could thrive in spaces that celebrated what we offered.

But the common imagery of retired women did not reflect my current reality—smiling grandmothers with silver hair surrounded by grandkids, puttering in a flower garden, reading a novel in a chaise at the beach, or standing on the deck of a cruise ship beside a presumably retired husband. These outdated stereotypes portrayed women as passive grandparents on cruises—not active, independent individuals shaping our own journeys.

As a childfree woman in my early fifties whose typical Colorado pursuits included hiking, camping, skiing, and cycling, I saw little of myself in those images. I did not hope to settle into a hushed, passive version of retirement. And no children, as it turned out, meant no grandchildren.

In the Netflix series *Secrets of the Blue Zones*, octogenarians in Okinawa, Japan, talk about "ikigai," a sense of purpose that makes life worth living. Okinawans claim that finding one's ikigai is the secret to longevity and well-being. I felt intrigued by the idea of uncovering that intersection of talent, interest, and what the world needed. Though, on paper, I was well-suited for my career, a true sense of purpose eluded me during my working life. In the years leading up to retirement, I devoured books, articles, and online tests in search of my own dharma, raison d'être, ikigai…my *why*.

While working, I often imagined leaving project management for something creative and soulful, in a part-time capacity—a lifestyle coach, hypnotherapist, death doula, or grant writer. I considered earning enough to cover the healthcare costs my full-time job provided, my own version of the Barista FIRE movement where people trade high-stress careers for something more relaxed. But I also did not want to spend time or money training for a second career, only to discover I did not like it. What if my fleeting thoughts about seeking this second, soulful career were simply about crafting a more acceptable narrative, something that sounded more noble than, "I want the flexibility to do other things"?

Over the years in Colorado, I had met women with steady careers in dental hygiene, sales, or customer service who longed to transition into second careers that impassioned them—becoming a reiki master, opening a Pilates studio, designing jewelry, or guiding outdoor adventures. I envied the zeal of these highly specialized women who found their callings and pursued them with a Bukowski-esque, "Find what you love and let it kill you" intensity. Their passions were not mere interests; they were obsessions—something they had to do. But I had never found anything I loved enough to let it kill me, metaphorically speaking. I respect the idea to "Follow your bliss," but the bumper-sticker glosses over the rest of Joseph Campbell's work, chock-full of threshold guardian warnings.

I felt more like a dilettante, dabbling in acrylic painting, traditional astrology, web analytics, or home design software while others seemed fueled by clear passions. Though there were plenty of activities I enjoyed and pastimes that brought me satisfaction, none consumed me with a singular devotion. I liked baking bread, but not enough to do it multiple times a day. I appreciated design and decor but had no desire to work in those fields. I was borderline obsessive with fitness and nutrition, but I could never stomach clients who refused to change bad habits. And while I adored animals, I had no interest in spending my days collecting samples of their blood and urine.

I love the opening monologue of the *Seinfeld* episode "The Suicide," when Jerry reminisces about hearing tests at school. He describes being ushered into a soundproof Airstream trailer, putting on headphones, and then being instructed to push a button whenever he heard a beep:

> I wanted them to come over to me after the hearing test and say, "We think you may have something close to super hearing. What you heard was a cotton ball touching a piece of felt. We're sending the results to Washington. We'd like you to meet the president."

Not unlike Jerry, I wanted to believe my disparate skills, preoccupations, and eccentricities would coalesce into a calling where I was not just needed but indispensable. My calling would be noble, yet I would be well-compensated. It would carry a modicum of prestige yet be slightly inaccessible—maybe even clandestine! But what exactly is the Venn diagram for a middle-aged analytical shapeshifter with a dark wit and a penchant for identifying Commonwealth accents?

Likes...Totally

Instead of turning my life over to an all-consuming passion, I started with something accessible: likes. While still working, I began keeping a List of Likes, no matter how odd or specific, in my iPhone Notes app. I paid attention to moments when time passed quickly, when I felt fully engaged, or when an activity left me feeling energized rather than depleted. I cobbled together questions from books, articles, and Pinterest pins I had accumulated over the years while trying to identify that noble calling, searching for my unique gifts.

- What energizes me?
- What calms me?
- What did I love to do as a child?
- What are my best childhood memories?
- What are my favorite memories with Scott? With friends?
- What have I been so engrossed in that I forgot to eat?
- What made me (almost) late for a meeting?

- What stories do my bookshelves, digital libraries, saved articles, and Pinterest boards tell?
- What would I do more of if not for the hassle?
- What classes would I like to take?
- Where do I nerd out?
- What quirks are unique to me?

I gave myself free rein when identifying likes—a like could be as small as sipping rooibos tea from my favorite mug or as random as repurposing old jewelry I no longer wore. Some were broad and others were hyper-specific. Some of my likes included granny hobbies—baking bread, making soup, and playing piano—all activities I found calming and grounding.

Other items on the list such as "Being around dogs" or "*Alice in Wonderland*" described interests, curiosities, or experiences. Some of my happiest memories involved traveling with Scott in Europe—sitting in a café, sipping wine after a museum visit, observing a local culture, and reflecting and sharing impressions of what we had seen. That particular moment may be hard to replicate on demand, but it weaves together so many of my likes—art and beauty, meaningful connection, travel, and the small thrill of ordering wine in a foreign language.

My List of Likes grew to include the following:

- High altitude hiking
- Running on packed snow
- Skiing corduroy midweek on a bluebird day
- Esoteric podcasts during solo gravel rides
- Esprit de corps of my cycling group along the trail in matching kits
- Swimming
- Bikram-style yoga
- Camping

- Observing wild animals in nature
- Being around dogs
- Eating good dark chocolate
- Sipping wine with Scott in a European café after a museum
- Observing cultural nuances while traveling
- Practicing French and Spanish on Duolingo
- Learning foreign words with no English equivalent
- Preparing a meal for family or friends
- Dedicating an afternoon to a complex recipe
- Assembling kitchen sink burritos for hikes or ski days
- Baking bread
- Burning scented candles
- Incorporating vintage finds into existing decor
- Upcycling or repurposing forgotten items
- The *New York Times* Connections puzzle
- Playing Beethoven on my weighted keyboard
- Watching clandestine series or movies
- Capsule wardrobes and tiny homes
- Dressing up
- Unpacking, cleaning, and tidying after travel
- Organizing, streamlining, and decluttering
- Personality categorizing, e.g., Myers-Briggs, traditional astrology, Big Five
- Reading about arcane topics
- Writing about my dreams
- *Alice in Wonderland*
- The Droste effect, mise en abyme, fractals, Fibonacci sequence, and recursion

To this list, I would later add "In-person painting classes," "Design and create a dress," and "Pickleball," not necessarily activities I knew I would enjoy but wanted to try. During Covid, for example, I took a painting class that did not hit the mark—its Zoom format made me feel as though I was still at work and did not offer the escape I hoped for, though I wanted to revisit painting. Though they helped guide me toward identifying likes, I did not include activities I was already doing in service to building and strengthening community, such as my neighborhood book club, volunteering, or traveling to visit family and friends.

When I examined my list more closely, I noticed that my likes naturally fell into categories:

Pleasure

Pleasures are small, fleeting indulgences—like eating dark chocolate or lighting a scented candle. They bring delight in the moment but are not substantial enough to build a life around. Many have tried, of course, but overindulgence in pleasure often leads to compulsion or addiction. Even the dictionary defines pleasure as "frivolous amusement," reminding us that while it has its place, it is not the foundation of lasting fulfillment.

Gratification

Gratification, unlike pleasure, involves effort and reward. Baking bread or completing the *New York Times* Connections puzzle brings me gratification as there is a sense of accomplishment attached. These activities often engage skills or strategy, and their rewards—though satisfying—tend to be external and short-lived. Gamification capitalizes on this concept, turning ordinary tasks into more engaging challenges by offering badges, points, or progress markers. While gratification is motivating, it does not provide the deeper sense of meaning that some pursuits offer.

Fulfillment

Fulfillment goes beyond gratification—it carries a sense of meaning and contribution. A year prior to retirement, I began volunteering one evening a week in the Emergency Department (ED) of our local hospital. My friend's mom, also a dog lover, believed I would enjoy it. The volunteer coordinator had decorated her office in an *Alice in Wonderland* theme, which I took as a sign that I belonged there. Though I would not describe filling medical supply carts as joyful, its necessity and simplicity have a Zen quality. At the end of my shift, I feel something deeper. I know I have played a role, albeit small, in supporting the technicians, nurses, and doctors on the front lines. That knowledge—that I have made someone's day slightly better—brings a sense of fulfillment. It connects me to a greater purpose that lingers far longer than the fleeting rewards of pleasure.

Joy

Joy is different from all the others—it is spontaneous and deeply emotional. It can strike in an instant, sparked by beauty, connection, or a sense of awe. Unlike pleasure or gratification, joy is not something we can manufacture or pursue directly. We remember moments of joy and may try to recreate them, but joy's elusive nature means it exists only in the present. Perhaps that is why I feel joy around dogs—they don't dwell on the past or anticipate the future. Dogs are happy right now. And right now.

I knew that retirement, in its ideal form, should include all of these—pleasure, gratification, fulfillment, and joy. The first two, I could likely generate daily—perhaps even multiple times a day if I wanted to. But if I built my days solely around eating dark chocolate, burning scented candles, and dutifully checking off Duolingo and piano practice, the novelty would wear thin—as would our chocolate supply. Real satisfaction would come not just from momentary pleasures, but from distilling what brought me fulfillment and joy—and expanding upon it in ways that felt meaningful.

Beneath each of my likes was a pattern, a reason they resonated so strongly. Was it creativity, a sense of connection, or the pursuit of knowledge? As I examined the activities, experiences, and moments that consistently brought me pleasure, gratification, fulfillment, and joy, I realized they were not just random preferences—they were signposts pointing toward something deeper. In listing what I liked, I not only identified hobbies or pastimes, but I also uncovered the foundation of what mattered most to me. To build a life that felt both meaningful and sustaining, I needed to go deeper—to articulate the core values underpinning my joy and fulfillment.

Defining My Core Values

Decades ago, while working with a career coach, I learned that choosing a career aligned with my core values would bring deeper satisfaction than a career that merely sounded prestigious or matched my area of aptitude. Now, I wondered, *Could that same approach guide me in this next phase? Could identifying my core values help me uncover my purpose, or at the very least, lead me to cultivate a more intentional path?*

Core values—also called intrinsic values—are valued for their own sake, without external rewards. You would still care about this value on a deserted island where nobody else would notice. Intrinsic values form the foundation of ethics and can include things like spirituality, justice, status, fun, pleasure, knowledge, or security. *Psychology Today* defines values as "an enduring belief upon which a person acts."

Extrinsic values, in contrast, are external rather than essential or inherent. They depend on others noticing or validating. Extrinsic motivators can be tangible, like money or cookies, or intangible, like compliments or fame. The distinction is that extrinsic motivators can be reduced to something intrinsic. Pursuing wealth—an extrinsic motivator—may satisfy intrinsic values such as freedom or security. Eating a cookie provides pleasure, and reading a book leads to knowledge.

So, how did I determine my core values? Online tests, of course! I took three.

Barrett Values Assessment (BVA)

This quick five-minute test ($19.95) grouped my values into seven categories resembling chakras in an hourglass—Contribution, Collaboration, Alignment, Evolution, Performance, Relationships, and Viability. The results, sent immediately, included two worksheets and self-reflection exercises.

www.valuescenter.com

Clear Thinking Intrinsic Values Test

A more in-depth twenty-minute assessment that ranked my values in order and categorized them into Universal, Community, and Self-Based values.

www.clearerthinking.org

Personal Values Test

A simple, fast-clicking exercise that ranked my top five values in less than five minutes—no personal information required.

www.personalvalu.es

I printed the BVA worksheets and crossed out values that did not resonate, refining my list until I was left with values that felt most meaningful. If I could align my likes and the activities I wanted to try in retirement with my core values, could I design a way of being that suited me? I reworked the values to reflect areas of focus. For example, both family and friendships represented loved ones with whom I wanted to spend more time, so "relationships" became my word to describe that core value. Creative projects brought me joy and fulfillment, so "joy and creativity" became another. To bring my values to life, I added verbs to each and created four categories, plus a bonus one for good measure:

- Promoting Health and Wellness
- Expanding and Strengthening Relationships
- Fostering Joy and Creativity
- Making the World a Better Place
- Et Pourquoi Pas! (And Why Not!)

Promoting Health and Wellness

Health and wellness are not optional—without them, retirement is merely survival. Imagine working for thirty or forty years, saving a portion of your paycheck every two weeks to fund retirement, and then just prior to retirement being diagnosed with heart disease or cancer!

I cherish my health, and I make it a daily priority to maintain, if not improve, it. I am fortunate to be as healthy as I am, and I do everything in my power to avoid the heart disease and lung cancer that run in my family. I enjoy being in nature, so many of my activities inherently involve fitness. For decades, I fit an active lifestyle into workdays—running after calls and doing barre workouts before dinner—while weekends and vacations gave me space to immerse myself in the outdoors.

With my newfound leisure, I had new ideas: swimming more regularly as a possible replacement for running, learning pickleball for its social aspects, and training within my women's cycling group to graduate from slower green to longer, faster blue gravel rides. I also wanted to deepen my commitment to wellness through better stretching, longer meditations, dry brushing, and other practices that I finally had time to incorporate into my routine.

Expanding and Strengthening Relationships

Scott is an only child, and because we do not have children, we make considerable efforts to stay connected with friends and family, wherever they are. We travel to see friends who have moved to new cities. During the holidays, we return to California to spend time with friends and Scott's extended family, and I regularly visit my immediate and extended family spread along the West Coast. Not only do we enjoy seeing the people we love, but we are also investing in our futures, strengthening existing connections as our lives change.

According to the Myers-Briggs test, I land somewhere between extrovert and introvert, leaning slightly toward introvert. I process the world through internal thinking—turning ideas over in my mind, observing and analyzing in fits and starts. Still, life has nudged me toward extroversion. I have moved across companies, cities, states—even a country—where I knew no one. I strike up conversations, show up solo, and say yes to invitations. And afterward, more than once, I have taken a nap in my car.

When we moved from California to Colorado, my massage therapist told me, during my first oracle card reading, to "notice the gifts," "be still," and "find my tribe." She said I needed to build more relationships beyond couple friendships. Though I maintained my California friendships via text, I knew I could do more.

Previous moves had taught me a strange lesson: to make friends before I needed them. Unpacking, acclimating to a new job, and finding a dentist and hairdresser in a new city are exhausting and time-consuming tasks. Before, I had made the mistake of procrastinating joining groups and making friends until I had settled, and before I knew it, months passed. By then, I felt lonely and isolated, like the only person catching up to make friends. The idea of finding my tribe resonated. I wanted to form new local friendships, reconnect with old ones scattered across the U.S., and spend time with my sister.

Jean-Paul Sartre said, "Hell is other people." And while this might feel true on crowded freeways or in packed Trader Joe's parking lots, the opposite is just as real—without human connection, we struggle. It is the reason Chuck built a raft in *Castaway* as well as why Robert talked to mannequins in *I Am Legend*.

Social isolation and loneliness pose a threat to both physical and mental health. Social isolation means not having relationships, nor contact with or support from others, whereas loneliness means the feeling of being alone, disconnected, or not close to others, even if people are in proximity. According to the CDC, social isolation is not just lonely—it is dangerous. It raises the risk of heart disease, stroke, and type 2 diabetes. Social isolation contributes to depression, anxiety, suicidal thoughts, and even dementia. It can shorten our lives and diminish their quality.

Greater Good Magazine says that social connections improve well-being across cultures and that relatedness is one of three basic psychological needs. If we do not cultivate social connections, we not only risk our health—we risk the joy of this next phase of life. Without the daily built-in interactions with colleagues and clients in retirement, it becomes even more important to intentionally build new relationships to maintain a sense of community and belonging. I enjoy my own company. I feel perfectly comfortable in the backyard under my umbrella with a book or cycling solo along gravel roads, but I included "Strengthening and Expanding Relationships" as one of my four categories because science says I will be happier and healthier spending time with others.

Fostering Joy and Creativity

After reflecting on my likes, I had a solid idea of the differences between pleasure, gratification, fulfillment, and joy. I had come to believe that, as a society, we often chase fleeting pleasures or instant gratification but less often cultivate activities that create space for genuine joy or lead to lasting fulfillment. In the past year, I asked a few friends, "What brings you joy?" I was continuously struck at how difficult it was to get answers. They easily provided examples of pleasure or gratification; providing examples of joy, however, was more difficult. With more time and flexibility, I could finally prioritize the experiences that nourish me and intentionally bring joy and creativity into my life.

Making the World a Better Place

I know early retirement is out of reach for many, something I do not take lightly. I wanted to be thoughtful about how I spent this time and reflect on why I wanted to give back. For me, making the world a better place meant embracing small, everyday acts of kindness. With more time in my life, I could focus on these simple but meaningful gestures.

I had already begun walking adoptable dogs at a local shelter. Our dog, Motu, passed in 2017, and due to frequent travel, we were not looking for another. Instead, the animal shelter provided my fur therapy; each week, I walked large-breed dogs for twenty minutes in the grass along the reservoir, where the dogs and I observed American White Pelicans, Cormorants, Snowy Egrets, and Canadian geese. I snapped a picture of each dog and posted them to the socials, sharing their joyful, tongue-out moments and quirky names—Paul Hollywood, Lady Wigglalot, Tom Yum, and Sharknado. Friends and family looked forward to these posts, and I felt a sense of connection through those joyful, derpy dog faces.

My duties while volunteering in the Emergency Department (ED) included filling blanket warmers and restocking linen cupboards, medical carts, and gloves. It was a surprisingly soothing experience, given the high-energy nature of the ED. In my career, I was used to making constant decisions and listening to clients throughout my day. But in the ED, the simple act of replenishing supplies offered a sense of calm and reassurance that the virtual nature of my workday did not. After each shift, I came home with a deep sense of peace and restfulness. It was a fulfilling break from my routine, and I highly recommend it. These acts, both big and small, helped make the world a little better, and I wanted to find additional ways to contribute.

Et Pourquoi Pas!

This was a fun name I created for a bonus category in which to lump all the activities that did not fit within the other four. This category includes eccentric ideas that piqued my curiosity. There was a lottery thought experiment I wanted to try. I thought about buying a durian—a tropical fruit with a polarizing taste and smell cultivated in Indonesia—to share during book club. Its purported vanilla custard and roasted garlic flavor plus sweaty-gym-socks-meets-sautéed-onions aroma intrigued me. I even considered going to a shooting range. This category created space for whimsy and experimentation, a reminder that not every pursuit needed to be practical. Some could exist simply for the thrill of trying something new.

Side-stepping the pressure to identify a singular passion—and instead focusing on what brought me pleasure, satisfaction, fulfillment, and joy—introduced unexpected clarity. Distilling what truly mattered into actionable core values helped me align my time and energy with meaning. But even with that clarity, I still craved a sense of intention and cohesion. The next step was to establish a structure—something that could give my days a sense of rhythm and meaning.

Four

Mid-Lifery

As I stepped away from something familiar without yet knowing what lay ahead, I felt unsettled, disoriented, and yet maybe, subtlety, full of possibility. I had not found a name for this liminal space I would inhabit. Retirement sounded too inactive. Sabbatical? Not really—I had no desire to return to project management. Act II? Deuxième partie?

Unlike launching a career where well-worn paths exist—earn a degree, land an entry-level job, gain experience—there was no clear guide for career culminations, especially a decade before traditional retirement age. Just as I initially had no blueprint for rebalancing my IRA from growth to income, I also had no blueprint for rebalancing my days from working to…not. Its absence left me both disquieted and oddly exhilarated.

Though some women leave careers in their forties and fifties with a clear sense of purpose, for many leaving a career is just one chapter in a broader mid-life narrative of upheaval. In mid-life, we may grapple with multiple transitions, caught between the undertow of uncertainty and the horizon of reinvention—a move to a new city, a medical diagnosis or recovery, the death of a partner, or the end of a long-term relationship.

Many women navigate empty nests—what author Gretchen Rubin calls an "Open Door," a metaphor that emphasizes possibility over loss. And all of us seemed to be unmoored in the murky waters of perimenopause, stranded between a dearth of medical education and a tsunami of online confusion and rage.

So, yeah, vibes get weird.

I had heard some retired people say they did not know where the time went and could not imagine how they ever fit work into their schedules, but I wanted to know. I wanted to pivot if my days began to dissolve into endless bread and cookie baking, obsessive organizing, or worse—hours lost to Reddit, Facebook's Dull Women's Group, or…video games.

I thrived on structure, and throughout my career, I had been disciplined and outcome-oriented, a mindset that was not going to vanish just because Outlook Calendar had. As a project manager, I spent a career planning outcomes and holding people accountable, ensuring they took the steps required to reach their goals. I did not just believe in good habits, small steps, and manageable chunks—I had been paid to live them.

Though my habits and structure had served me well in my career, I suspected that some of these traits might become obstacles in a less structured life. My tendency toward regimentation worked professionally, but it made me wonder if I could embrace a dynamic schedule. Could I be flexible when Scott updated our shared Google calendar? Shift gears (pun intended) to join a spontaneous gravel ride on an unseasonably warm February day? Would I have the courage to paint badly when inspiration struck?

Beyond being regimented, I could be a relentless taskmistress (Where are my Capricorns?), focused on the instant gratification of checking items off to-do lists rather than the deeper, more sustaining fulfillment of creative projects. I had gamified some of my hobbies—practicing piano, learning French, and re-learning Spanish—collecting virtual gems, trophies, and Duolingo streaks. I often wondered if I was truly learning and growing, or if these were simply distractions feeding my ego's need to feel productive.

In retirement, would I pursue these and more, only to find myself isolated and disillusioned, drowning in completed mirror barre workouts, Duolingo badges, and checklist after completed checklist, without any real connection to my soul? I needed to find my natural cadence, exploring my curiosities and pastimes in a spirit of growth, without cheapening my days and suffering from gold star syndrome.

I continued to ask myself the same question I asked when we still lived in California:

What would a fulfilling retirement look like?

And then, another thought surfaced. I had spent years managing outcomes—why not manage retirement like a project? What if my final deliverable was not working software, but rather, a fulfilling retirement?

Whether building battle tanks, homes, or software, every project requires balancing three key constraints: scope, time, and cost. Scope sets the project's goal—like developing a website with a navigation menu, search function, and login. Time is the agreed upon deadline—say, to deliver the project by May 1. Cost reflects the resources needed to complete it. The end result? A tested, working product.

For retirement, scope would be my List of Likes. Time would be my first twelve months of retirement. Cost—well, that I would manage as I went along, month by month. And while I would never, ever recommend managing costs on the fly with a software project, I was not building software—I was building a life. And more importantly, I was not billing hourly.

I felt energized! Retirement, for all its freedom, also comes with uncertainty, and the idea of treating it like a project gave me a familiar sense of control. I was not just stepping away from work—I was stepping toward something intentionally designed, something I would (hopefully) find rewarding.

I formatted my list into a spreadsheet (I do love a spreadsheet!) with Activity (scope) in the first column, sourced from my List of Likes. Across the top, I created five columns—my Core Values—and marked each activity with an X in the relevant columns. The last column included the Timeline.

I assigned each Activity to a month, a timeline not only to make myself accountable, but also to pace myself and prevent burnout. I assigned easier, task-based activities to January and February. Just like a software project, I knew that small wins fueled by enthusiasm in the first couple of months would build confidence and create momentum. More ambitious activities, as well as those that required better weather, I assigned to later months. August through December, I left blank to permit space for change—I knew from actual projects that incomplete activities would spill into the following month. Some I would abandon, others would be blocked by circumstances beyond my control (eww), and I would inevitably add new activities.

Tᴛ Activity	Better World	Wellness & Fitness	Relationships	Joy & Creativity	Timeline
Stretching and dry-brushing		x			January
Longer meditations		x		x	January
Restart giving blood regularly	x				January
Restyle bar cart				x	January
Pickleball lessons		x	x		January
Practice feng shui				x	January
Order reusable hankies	x				January
Pair Apple watch/Garmin computer		x			February
Start composting	x				February
Resume swimming		x			February
Piano lessons				x	February
Join a yoga studio		x			February

While this format gave me a clear sense of direction by defining the scope and timeline, I needed a way to bring that vision into my daily life and incorporate it into my routines.

Every. Damn. Day.

In contrast to my super-commute years in California, due to shorter commutes initially and then remote work after the pandemic, moving to Colorado had allowed me to spend more time doing what I loved. Each morning, I woke up early without an alarm, made a cup of tea, and wrote in the quiet stillness. Breakfast was wholesome and consistent—organic rolled oats with oat milk, frozen fruit, and nut butter. Then, I went to yoga or hit the trails.

If tea, journaling, and exercise began my day with ritualistic intention, my routines in the evenings after work equally provided structure and gratification. I naturally eased into a slower rhythm, starting meal preparation around four o'clock and showering before dinner to instill a sense of relaxation. I practiced Duolingo and then meditated before climbing into bed to read. These were not just routines but intentional practices that grounded me in the life I wanted to create, ensuring my days reflected what mattered most.

These consistent actions—known as anchor habits in behavioral psychology and habit formation science—are small, meaningful rituals that tend to happen no matter what else is going on. BJ Fogg, a Stanford behavioral scientist and author of *Tiny Habits*, writes about anchor moments as existing behaviors to which one attaches a new habit—for example, adding a new habit of flossing onto the existing habit of brushing your teeth. Anchor habits do not need to be ambitious or productive—but they need to matter to us. More than items on a to-do list, they serve as emotional touchstones, reinforcing our well-being and aligning our days with our priorities and values.

As wellness blogger Ashley Pitt notes on her blog *A Lady Goes West*, positive anchor habits help us feel grounded—especially when life feels unpredictable. They tether us to a sense of self. This is why anchor habits can be particularly valuable in retirement: They offer a sense of continuity, easing the transition into a new phase of life. So, how did I identify my anchor habits? This time, there was no online test—I jotted down general habits from a typical workday.

≈ 6:00 - Wake up
6:00 - 7:00 - Tea, journaling, breakfast
7:00 - 8:00 - Exercise
8:00 - 4:30 - Work
4:30 - 5:30 - Dinner prep, piano, shower
5:30 - 7:00 - Dinner + TV + cleanup
7:00 - 8:30 - Duolingo, meditation, reading in bed
≈ 8:30 - Sleep

Recognizing the stability of these rituals, I began to explore how anchor habits in this new phase aligned with what mattered to me. After decades of structuring my days around meetings, deadlines, and deliverables, I found comfort in creating a new kind of schedule—one built around what nourished me. Just as I once followed a workday rhythm, I began to examine what a meaningful daily rhythm could look like in retirement.

Drinking Tea

Buddhist monk and activist Thích Nhất Hanh spoke of the practice of drinking tea slowly and reverently, practicing mindfulness while drinking it. He guides us to be present in the here and now because tea, like life, will be gone before we know it. I wanted to spend at the very least fifteen minutes of my day drinking tea mindfully and being present—after that first cup, I could mindlessly slurp in my attempt to solve the *New York Times* Connections puzzle in reverse rainbow order.

Morning Quiet Time

Without weekday eight o'clock start times for conference calls and email replies, my practice of writing in journals and reading articles online expanded well into the morning. While I drank tea and wrote, Scott drank coffee and read. We cherish our quiet mornings together, sitting mostly in silence.

Exercise

I was no longer required to squeeze exercise in between calls or just before dinner, so I could take a long walk or a four-hour bike ride when the weather cooperated. This would expand to include resuming a hot yoga practice, swimming, training for longer and faster rides, and finally, learning to clip in.

≈ 6:00 - Wake up

6:00 - 9:00 - Tea + morning quiet time

9:00 - 2:00 - Exercise + activities

2:00 - 4:30 - To-do's + Nap

4:30 - 5:30 - Dinner prep + shower

5:30 - 7:00 - Dinner + TV + cleanup

7:00 - 9:00 - Evening quiet time + reading in bed

≈ 9:00 - Sleep

When I stepped back to review my new list, I felt a quiet happiness. It preserved the comfort and stability of my anchor habits—the morning and evening rituals that bookended my days—while remaining flexible enough to support the projects and experiences I would explore in this new phase.

I was embarking on an experiment. It included my List of Likes—not a single, all-consuming passion, but a humble collection of ideas that brought me pleasure, meaning, and fulfillment—grounded in my core values. The timeline would help me pace myself through the first year, and my anchor habits would serve as a daily container for purpose—scaffolding for my days, maintaining a level of continuity from my working life as I added new pursuits.

I also created a shared calendar. Scott and I share a car, and while working, I typically used the car only on weekends. I did not want to throw our lives into chaos with my new flexibility, so I created an online calendar to communicate and manage the use of our car. It was also immensely helpful for reminding us of travel, appointments with contractors, trash and recycling collection days, and sending birthday wishes.

I was not just organizing time or curating enjoyable pastimes; I was opening myself up to growth, creating space for discovery, and welcoming the unfamiliar parts of myself.

Artifacts

List of Likes
Core Values
Timeline
Anchor Habits
Shared Calendar

I had developed these artifacts to support me through the first twelve months of retirement by the time I announced my retirement to my employer. As I transitioned projects to colleagues and prepared clients for my departure, they admitted that they were both happy for me and envious, but also curious.

"What will you do?" asked my client.

"I created a spreadsheet," I said. "I started with a list of the things I wanted to do but never had time for while working, and then I separated them into categories. But also, just to make sure I don't burn myself out in the first two months, I spread those activities out over a year into a rough timeline—like a project roadmap. I want to write about my journey, assumptions, learnings, and what I wish I had known…stuff like that."

Most people laughed, albeit in a friendly, amused way.

"I guess that makes sense, a project manager managing retirement like a project—with lists, spreadsheets, timelines, and a calendar."

Five

January

- **Practice feng shui**
- **Expand self-care rituals**
- **Make regular blood donations**
- **Adopt sustainable habits**
- **Take pickleball lessons**

Though my last day of work was December 14, when people asked about retirement, I said, "This is Christmas break. Ask me on January 2." We were in Palm Desert for the holidays, escaping the deepest winter cold of Colorado, spending time with California friends and family.

So, how did January 2 feel? Nothing short of spectacular, exactly as I imagined! I hiked through the desert with Scott, where we had deep, uninterrupted conversations about the connections in our lives, our blind spots, and tacos.

I changed my LinkedIn profile from "Software Project Manager" to "Exploring Part II." To the socials, I posted an ungainly self-portrait with a rhetorical question, "Guess who has two thumbs and is not working on her birthday?!" I felt shot out of a cannon, free from the daily confines of conference calls and status reports, ready to devour my newfound freedom.

Once we returned home from California after the holidays, I felt elated to return to our space—newly retired and operating on my own agenda. In my bed, surrounded by a stillness I had never felt, I awoke in my home as a retired person for the first time. No longer squeezed by arbitrary deadlines, I would have time and room. I was torn between savoring the tranquility of the morning and harnessing the energy of the new year to complete everything on my Return to Colorado list.

Cleaning and organizing has been my ritual of symbolic order, a way to transmute nervous energy and unpredictability into something visible, and productive. I have read Marie Kondō's book *The Life-Changing Magic of Tidying Up* twice. After unpacking and doing laundry, I consolidated rolls of Christmas wrapping paper, retrieved plants from friends who watered them while we were away, and exchanged some Christmas presents for smaller sizes. We usually emptied the pantry and fridge before we left, which gave me the perfect excuse to deep-clean the refrigerator and wipe down the cupboards, drawers, and pantry. There is a particular satisfaction in the simple, meditative acts of vacuuming crumbs from corners, wiping sticky rings of oil, vinegar, and honey from the pantry shelves—residue that forms no matter how carefully I wipe each bottle. I take solace in these cycles, emptying out to welcome in.

The first three days at home were a whirlwind of all-day GSD (get sh*t done), bookended by quiet mornings and evenings in the living room with Scott. I allowed myself that frenzied pace—permission to clean the slate for what was next. I have always tackled the hardest things first. As a child who didn't like broccoli, I ate it first. "Get it over with," I'd tell myself. But now that I could fill my plate with mostly things I loved, I almost didn't know where to begin. I wanted to write, but I felt creatively parched, ideas evaporating the moment I made time and space for them. Still, I reminded myself that, five years ago, I would have given anything to be here—uncertain, but free.

Sometimes when things feel absurd or unsteady, I imagine myself as Alice in Wonderland. There were no meetings, no deadlines, and no map. It was absurd to be fifty-three, retired, and sitting in a sparkling clean home, wondering, *What now?* Maybe the question was not a crisis but an invitation to follow my curiosity, to get lost, and to grow strange and brave again.

Having Feng (Shui) Yet?

I added "Practice feng shui" (fŭng′ shwā′) to January because it felt like the perfect way to begin the new year, Fostering Joy and Creativity. I listen to the "Simple Shui" podcast with Amanda Gibby Peters—she even read one of my submitted questions on an episode! Her book, *Simple Shui for Every Day*, with its vibrant cover, has earned a spot on my coffee table. Amanda's approach is refreshingly practical rather than overly woo-woo, and her upbeat, cheerful demeanor makes her advice feel both accessible and motivating. She emphasizes enhancing a space's energy through small, intentional changes—clearing clutter, introducing color and live plants, improving light and airflow, and ensuring that everything we keep serves a purpose.

When I added "Practice feng shui" to my original list, I had not been specific, so by January, I no longer remembered what I had in mind. Instead, I followed Amanda's simple yet powerful recommendation to move twenty-seven things. The number twenty-seven, a multiple of nine, carries symbolic meaning: It represents power, manifestation, and completion. This practice frees up stagnant chi, allowing energy to circulate rather than settle among objects we have grown so used to that we barely notice them anymore. Best of all, it required no purchases, just a fresh perspective and a willingness to shift my surroundings.

No longer home to Zoom meetings and budget forecasts, my home office became my starting point, as it now served a different function— I would sit at my desk and write about retirement! This space represented how I had spent eight hours a day. Moving twenty-seven things was a prescriptive effort to release the repetitive energy of weekly reports and client calls and invite my own creative energy into a familiar environment. I cleared the shelves, dusted, and rearranged everything—decor and astrology books, scented candles, and climbing Golden Pothos in blue and white pots.

I hung my grandmother's watercolor painting that for too long sat propped up against the wall, and I culled unworthy focal points like a tired bell jar of wine corks. Though the quirky, whimsical items on the shelves were the same—a lifelike yellow Labrador statue, a blue peace sign hand gesture candle, and nested Russian Matryoshka dolls—they felt refreshed, as though twenty-seven items and their freed-up chi imbued my office with a playful spirit.

I then moved to the basement, removing items that remained after we organized the area prior to the holidays. I cut down and recycled cardboard boxes left over from Christmas. I hauled away a carload of clothes, shoes, and housewares and donated them to a local charity, and I dropped cans of paint at our local recycling facility. Our basement not only looked amazing but was in full feng shui compliance! Purging items from the basement may not seem like an activity that provides joy and creativity for everyone, but it did for me. I feel lighter when I have rescued a space from clutter to reveal its true purpose. The finished portion of the basement felt open and free, and the unfinished storage area was tidy and thoughtfully arranged.

Rhymes with Elf Lair

For me, the term "self-care" had been hijacked by retailers in their zeal to convince me to buy something—aromatherapy oils or lavender soy candles—when what I needed was a nap or a walk. Tired of reading about "self-care," I went about using "soul attention" when referring to embodied practices that encouraged stillness and presence. With more leisure time, I wanted to expand my soul attention to include dry brushing, thorough post-workout stretching sessions, and longer daily meditations. These three activities were in my Promoting Wellness and Fitness category.

Perhaps you're thinking, *Brooke. I get that you're not a quarterback en route to Disney World fresh off a Super Bowl win, but let me get this straight. After decades of working and years of super-commuting, your big foray into retirement leisure was…dusting shelves and exfoliating? No Mt. Whitney or El Capitan summit? No Camino de Santiago pilgrimage? No ashram for silent meditation?*

Retirement is a change. January, the dead of winter, represented a time for renewal, which was exactly the way I wanted to feel, anew and generative, flexible yet held. Though it was mundane, I chose to begin the year with embodied practices to gently remind my body that we were stepping into a new identity. My journey would not focus on Instagram-worthy bucket list items—I sought purpose at my own cadence. Besides, there would be plenty of time for epic hikes, pilgrimages, and silent retreats to make their way into my spreadsheet.

Fire…walk with me.

Dry brushing involves brushing the skin with a bristle brush to remove dead skin cells, typically prior to a shower or bath, resulting in softer skin. It stimulates the nervous system, feels invigorating, and offers immediate benefits without a learning curve. While you may have read the factoid that our bodies regenerate every seven years, according to WebMD, our skin cells regenerate every twenty-seven days. I didn't know that when I moved my twenty-seven objects to break up stagnant chi, but I smiled when I learned it later. My skin—my literal outer layer—had been renewing itself on the same feng shui rhythm I was trying to create in my home. January's theme was out-with-the-old, in-with-the-new, and dry brushing became a ritual that mirrored this shift.

It took only five minutes and required nothing more than a stiff-bristled brush, so it slid easily into my shower routine.

While working, I squeezed rides and runs between conference calls and then typically leaned against any convenient wall or countertop—often during conference calls—for twenty-second calf and quadricep stretches. I consistently incorporated these short stretches after cycling or running because whenever I forgot to stretch, I ached. But in my fifties, twenty-second stretches no longer served me. I awoke in the mornings, getting out of bed stiff and crunchy, wobbling back and forth like Frankenstein on tight Achilles tendons.

Free from conference calls, I began heading to our basement home gym, after a run or ride, for a thorough stretching session. It was only a matter of reminding myself to walk down to the basement, usually just after drinking a glass of water. The entire routine—techniques gathered from barre and yoga classes—only took about ten minutes, an easy commitment to undertake when I was already dressed in exercise clothing. Stretching in the cool basement with dimmed lights became more than a habit for maintaining flexibility, though flexibility is important. It grew into a way of allowing—allowing time to cool down, sprawl across the entire mat, breathe into the tightness and tension, and feel it transform into ease.

I have disgustingly, insanely good sleep hygiene. My early bedtime is legendary among friends and family, and they know that I will not answer a text or call after 8 p.m. For decades, they have known that I will not be available on school nights. If, on some rare occasion, we are still at the dinner table as the clock inches toward eight, it becomes increasingly difficult to stifle my yawns because my body expects to be in bed. "Oh, look. It's past Brookie's bedtime," they say. I credit my ability to consistently sleep between seven and nine hours to low caffeine intake, exercise, early dinners, regular bedtimes, and most importantly, a meditation practice.

I began meditating in 2002 after I read *Grow Younger, Live Longer: Ten Steps to Reverse Aging* by Deepak Chopra. I was working in Orange County and super-commuting, so during my lunch hour I drove to an empty shaded parking lot and reclined the car seat to meditate. To be still. Sometimes the meditation turned into a nap, which Deepak said was okay. This simple act left me calmer yet with more energy, so it became a daily habit.

More recently, just prior to bed, I typically meditate while sitting in a chair in the dark with noise-canceling earbuds, listening to a brown noise playlist. In retirement, I envisioned myself practicing longer meditations during the day, likely after a run or ride. I enjoy my state of mind after a workout. Meditation seems to extend the endorphin-induced calmness I got from tiring myself during exercise. It also decreases the stress hormone cortisol, which can increase during high-intensity workouts. For these reasons, I wanted to incorporate longer meditations into my routine and reclaim more stillness.

I have experimented with guided meditations and various forms of music from the Calm app as well as Spotify binaural beats, meditation, and color noise playlists. My objective during meditation is to empty my mind. For a time during Covid, I did meditate for longer stretches, and I am not sure why I stopped. Longer meditations make ordinary life feel magical. They make me more aware of synchronicities, my dreams become more vivid, and they bring a greater sense of awe, connection, and wonder in the natural world.

Sometimes magical things happen, like the time I saw three bull elk with velvety antlers outside my office window, even though at the time I lived far from open spaces. A stranger walked by and high-fived me for no obvious reason other than it was a beautiful spring day in Colorado. Or maybe he was high. On a pedestrian overpass, I saw a wizard—purple robe, long, white beard, and a pointy hat. I am not saying meditation caused these things to happen, but I think it contributes to noticing and appreciating them. I longed to return to that magic.

During my first month of retirement, however, I found myself repeatedly forgetting to meditate during the day. When evening rolled around, I was either too tired or too eager to climb into bed with a book to muster the patience for a longer session. I also discovered a surprising obstacle—my own digestion. The gurgling, churning sounds of my stomach processing dinner—known as borborygmi—proved to be an oddly persistent distraction, making it difficult to settle my mind.

James Clear, in *Atomic Habits: Tiny Changes, Remarkable Results*, explains that for a new habit to stick, it must be obvious, attractive, easy, and satisfying. He also introduces the concept of "habit stacking," which capitalizes on the brain's tendency to link behaviors together, making it easier to adopt a new habit by anchoring it to an existing one.

Showering was already part of my routine, so I seamlessly linked it to dry brushing. Exercise was another ingrained habit, so stretching naturally followed. These small shifts wove themselves effortlessly into my routines. But longer meditations—despite being obvious, attractive, and satisfying—found themselves wedged between Duolingo lessons and reading in bed, utterly defenseless against the persistent gurgle of borborygmi.

I had no idea how much the year would reflect themes of stretching, stillness, and skin.

Bloody Good Cheetos and a Bit of Hanky-Panky

I had fallen out of the habit of donating blood due to gallbladder surgery the year prior, and if I am honest, the aggressive email campaigns from the collecting organization made me less than enthusiastic about donating again. But in January, I logged onto the portal and scheduled an appointment, which fell into my category Making the World a Better Place.

Making an appointment was easy as the portal allowed me to filter by location and date, so I could find an appointment within a mile or two of my home. After donating, I developed the habit of immediately scheduling my next appointment. Because the appointments can be no sooner than eight weeks apart, it is easy to find a convenient time and location. They offer a "fast track" option, a questionnaire completed the day of donations, which reduces the time it takes to donate.

I received texts from the collecting organization weeks after donating, notifying me that my blood had been given to someone in need. A simple act of donating—something that I had long forgotten about and did not miss—felt so impactful when I received those texts. And reading them brought me to tears every damn time! The employees were warm and friendly, and donating blood was the only occasion when I allowed myself to eat Cheetos or animal crackers. Do it for the snacks!

In my effort to Make the World a Better Place, I wanted to start composting. According to NPR, up to 40 percent of U.S. food ends up in landfills. While Scott and I are diligent about eating leftovers and minimizing food waste, the sheer volume of produce we consume means a daily pile of cilantro stems, citrus and melon rinds, squash peels, coffee grounds, and tea leaves. A few months ago, our city distributed composting bins and began biweekly pickups on recycling day, making it easy to start.

During dinner prep each night, I filled an empty yogurt or salad container with onion skins, old lettuce, cilantro stems, and cauliflower leaves (though, oddly, I have come across recipes for those!). After dinner, as Scott wiped down the countertops, I dumped the food scraps to the backyard compost bin. Scott grew tired of seeing food scraps in ugly to-be-recycled containers sitting on our otherwise clutter-free countertop and ordered a sleek countertop compost bin—functional and aesthetically pleasing. Instead of tossing scraps into the trash, we simply deposited them into the compost bin.

Our composting habit soon inspired other eco-friendly changes. Despite our efforts to reduce plastic—like buying reusable silicone lids, using containers instead of baggies, and shopping with reusable grocery bags—plastic still finds its way into our home. Frozen fruit, fresh produce, bulk grains, and dried goods are often packaged in plastic, and we cannot avoid it entirely. I saved plastic bags for dog poop bags when I walked ready-to-be-adopted shelter dogs. (Pro tip: Never use vented plastic grape bags for dog poop, a disaster waiting to happen!)

I discovered from Earth911.com that plastic bags and film could be recycled at grocery stores, and the Safeway I passed en route to the shelter had a recycling bin just inside the entrance. This quick detour added less than five minutes to my weekly drive home from the shelter. Do I trust that these bags are recycled rather than shipped overseas to be incinerated? I have no way of knowing. But I am hopeful that small steps like these make up a larger effort to reduce waste and protect our planet.

Our household was already pretty far down the road of eliminating disposable paper products. We stopped using paper plates years ago. I bought cute Swedish dishcloths for wiping counter tops, replaced paper napkins with washable cotton/linen dinner napkins, and stored rags under every sink and in the laundry and garage areas to drastically reduce our paper towel usage. Also in the category Making the World a Better Place, I wanted to adopt the sustainable habit of replacing facial tissue with washable hankies.

For skiing, hiking, and cycling I carried a handkerchief, one of my classic brightly colored paisley bandanas that are punishingly rough after several washings. After a few too many tissues in the pockets of my robe and running tights created messes in the washing machine, I decided I needed soft, washable hankies to stash in convenient locations for everyday use. I ordered four organic cotton hankies from Etsy.

Using reusable hankies was an unbelievably easy habit to adopt! I placed a hanky in my handbag, one in my robe, and I left one in a bathroom drawer to add to the pocket of whatever I was wearing that day—I assumed one would always be in the wash. Each time I touched the soft, organic cotton, I appreciated its texture and convenience. I also liked the idea of supporting an independent artisan instead of Kimberly-Clark or Procter & Gamble.

I added pickleball lessons to my list of activities largely because one of my neighbors mentioned how social it was—something I could add to both my Strengthening and Expanding Relationships and Promoting Health and Wellness categories. I figured the cute skirts were just a bonus! But I learned that most of the pickleball in my area takes place outdoors, which means lessons are largely seasonal and generally do not begin until April or May. I moved my pickleball lessons from January to April. Instead of dinking my way into the new year, I shelved my pickleball aspirations until spring—giving me just enough time to find the perfect cute skirt.

January Check-In

Practice feng shui √
Expand soul attention routines √
Make regular blood donations √
Adopt sustainable habits √
Take pickleball lessons ◯

I decided that, for each month, I would evaluate my efforts by creating a check-in and assign a checkmark to each completed activity and an empty circle to those left incomplete. I was off to a strong start for the year!

At least, that is what I thought at first. But as I began to dig into why I had chosen these activities in the first place, I realized I wanted my retirement to be purposeful—filled with creativity, gratitude, charity, and wellness. Was purchasing Etsy organic cloth hankies and practicing feng shui worthy of a year-long project?

I reminded myself that I had deliberately chosen January's activities because, in the past, ideas for personal creative projects often began with excitement, only to later dissolve when I felt discouraged because they were too ambitious or did not fit into my schedule. Managing projects taught me the value of small wins to build confidence and create momentum, especially in the beginning. Charles Duhigg explains this concept in *The Power of Habit*, writing that tiny bursts of dopamine from small victories fuel motivation, brighten our days, and pave the way for lasting change.

I knew that modest, positive changes would trigger a ripple effect of greater transformations. At least, intellectually I knew this. But, more often than not, I panicked, believing myself unqualified for my creative pursuits because I lacked advanced degrees and years of experience in the subject, or that they required more research. It was a classic perfectionism paradox. But then somewhere in the cold, dark comfort of January, I decided that overthinking and worrying about how other people defined qualifications was not a way for me to be, not anymore. If I was going to fail, I was going to fail spectacularly…in coordinated athleisure wear.

Six

February

- **Resume lap swimming**
- **Take piano lessons**
- **Sign up for a hot yoga trial**
- **Pair watch with bike computer**

Reflecting upon my small victories in January emboldened me to tackle more ambitious activities in February.

Resuming Childhood Hobbies

Swimming has often served as a sanctuary for me. I took swimming lessons as a child and passed the American Red Cross Level 6: Swimming and Skill Proficiency. My neighbor, a widowed nurse who worked nights, allowed me to swim in her pool whenever I wanted, without having to ask. She hated the idea of the pool going unused and only asked that I close the gate behind me when I left. After completing my assigned chores at home, our neighbor's pool became my solo summer escape where I counted laps under the sun, resting on the warm concrete between sets, flipping through Mademoiselle magazine. I dove for coins and hovered midway between the bottom and the surface of the pool, enjoying my underwater vantage point while gazing up at the sky, a beautiful blue that still reminds me of summer.

Though my love for swimming began in childhood, it was not until Scott and I visited California over the holidays that I felt the pull to return to it as part of my adult routine. Decades later, I found myself rediscovering this joy at the Palm Desert Aquatic Center. In the water, the first few strokes rinsed clutter from my brain as thoughts drifted from the mundane to a meditative rhythm. With each breath, my mind cleared space for creativity and calm. Swimming was more than exercise—it was therapy.

When we returned to Colorado after the holidays, I felt eager to resume lap swimming. In mid-February, I began a free one-week trial at our local recreation center. Once the trial ended, I joined the community center and began swimming three days a week, aligned with my category Promoting Health and Wellness.

An unexpected benefit of joining a community center was, well, community. I swam at roughly the same time each day, and in doing so, I began to recognize others who swam during the same hours. I learned their names and said hello if I saw them in adjacent lanes or in the locker room. They were either pleasantly surprised or deftly able to conceal their horror that I remembered their names and their stories. This led to short but pleasant conversations, and conversations with strangers—especially when you mostly listen—can be satisfying and informative.

These social connections are what *The Atlantic*'s Amanda Mull refers to as "weak ties" in her article "The Pandemic Has Erased Entire Categories of Friendship." Weak ties are people we see infrequently, near strangers with whom we share a certain familiarity. A weak tie might be a person we recognize at the gym, a barista who knows our usual order, or the owner of an Indian restaurant calling to confirm medium spice when our usual order is mild. These outer-circle relationships are essential to our health and well-being because they expand our world beyond our usual inner-circle and offer friendly, low-maintenance interactions that lift our moods.

When Covid eliminated both my commute and my local yoga studio, it left extra hours in my weekdays. In 2022, after a year of deliberating, as part of an intention to pursue creative projects, I purchased a weighted keyboard. The keys mimic the resistance and feel of playing an acoustic piano, making it a satisfying alternative. Not yet ready to commit to formal lessons, I downloaded the SimplyPiano app to my iPhone and instead committed to solo daily piano practice.

SimplyPiano listens to notes played, provides real-time feedback, and only advances the song when the notes are played correctly. While pricey for an app at $130 annually, it helped me pick up playing immediately. Within the Basics and Essentials I & II courses, I began learning chords and simple songs.

After a few weeks of practicing chords and song excerpts, I switched to the app's Play feature. This teaches full songs from a genre-sorted library at three levels of complexity: beginner, intermediate, and pre-advanced. Each song is divided into manageable sections to master before playing as a whole.

I started with beginner arrangements of popular songs like "Don't Stop Believin'" and "Sweet Caroline"—recognizable, if simplified, versions of songs I grew up with. Later, I moved on to beginner arrangements of classics like "Edelweiss" and "Amazing Grace." Playing "Edelweiss" felt nostalgic—I had learned the song in third grade, back when playing the wrong chord merited a bellow from the kitchen: "That's not right!" As I progressed, I tackled beginner arrangements of pieces by Beethoven and Bach, eventually moving to intermediate and pre-advanced versions.

I played in Scott's basement office, door closed, headphones plugged into the keyboard. Only the app and I knew when I hit the wrong notes. The black notes on a white background provided a clear structure, and with repetition, I could eventually play songs without errors. Some lessons gave me a score for accuracy and tempo, adding an element of gamified progress. Unlike activities such as acrylic painting, piano required little setup. There was no need to change into old clothes, haul out an easel, or face the intimidation of a blank canvas. In contrast to the canvases leaning against basement walls that bore witness to my struggles with wannabe Rothko-esque abstracts, piano also left no physical evidence of my artistic failures. There were no primitive attempts at color block triptychs waiting to be painted over, just a digital catalogue of songs.

But after two years with the app, I realized I had not legitimately learned to read or play music. I relied on gamified trial and error to find the correct keys, merely mimicking songs from muscle memory. Without the app, I could not play at all, and I felt neither musical nor artistic. When I reflected on why I had chosen piano as an adult, I realized I was drawn to its relative safety. Piano was a tidy, convenient pursuit. I could practice for thirty minutes between conference calls or just before dinner—a time when I would usually long for Friday and a glass of wine. Piano became another task to check, alongside Duolingo, meditation, and exercise.

I didn't want a task. I wanted to play.

In February, I set an intention to begin piano lessons with an instructor and learn to read and play music, part of Fostering Joy and Creativity. Finding a piano instructor, however, proved more challenging than expected. I completed inquiry forms on the websites of three local instructors. Two never responded, and the third—highly recommended by my neighbors—offered a schedule tailored to school-age children, with little flexibility for my travel needs. I decided to keep searching and ultimately did not begin lessons in February.

Hot Yoga and Cool Sensations

Prior to Covid, I regularly attended Bikram-style yoga—a sequence of twenty-six postures in a room heated to 105 degrees. Some postures, called asanas, are named after the animals they (somewhat) resemble—rabbit, camel, cobra, and eagle. Other asanas, like wind-relieving pose…not so majestic. The intense heat and humidity loosened my muscles as I transitioned from struggling through asanas to gliding through the sequence. The practice rooted me fully in the present and left me feeling light, floating from the studio, red-faced with wet hair and sweaty clothing. I missed it.

Eager to return to this transcendent routine, I created an account online and received a notice for a forty-dollar two-week trial. It sounded perfect, but with a trip to Florida planned in February, I decided to postpone the trial until March.

Scott had recently purchased a new Garmin bike computer, a GPS device equipped with bike-specific road mapping, performance monitoring, and power meters. Initially, I planned to pair my Apple Watch with Scott's old Garmin bike computer—until I realized I didn't care about anything it measured. My Apple Watch tracked distance, time, calories burned, and effort level—the road mapping might be cool, but I didn't want additional performance benchmarks.

Preparing for a ride already created a checklist of essentials: ensuring my tires were at the correct pressure; packing enough food and water for a two-to-four-hour ride; charging my phone, headphones, and bike lights; and liberally applying mineral high-SPF sunscreen and chamois butter. (Chamois butter is cream to prevent bum chafing. I prefer the cooling formula, likening it to a York Peppermint Patty and its cool "York Sensation.") Adding a bike computer to the mix felt burdensome. In the spirit of the Et Pourquoi Pas, I decided this item would not carry over to March and happily crossed it off my list.

February Check-In

Resume lap swimming √
Take piano lessons ◯
Sign up for a hot yoga trial ◯
~~Pair Garmin computer and Apple Watch~~

Seven

March

- **Take piano lessons**
- **Sign up for a hot yoga trial**
- **Make nutrition bars**
- **Design a pit bull button**

By March, I had fully instilled my post-work routines, a new normal that felt entirely natural. Over cups of warm tea, I read, wrote, and completed the *New York Times* Connections puzzle in the quiet winter early mornings. Fueled by bowls of overnight oats and fruit, I exercised mid-morning—running, swimming, even sometimes cycling on an unseasonably warm and sunny (week!) day. In the afternoons, I volunteered or focused on my activities. True to my habits, my evenings remained unchanged. The occasional trip to visit friends and family offered a welcome distraction, always followed by a deep appreciation for our beautiful surroundings, quiet home, and comforting routines when we returned.

One More Time with Feeling

In March, I resumed my search for a piano teacher and found an instructor who allowed me to purchase lessons in four-session blocks and schedule them at our convenience. We arranged a meet and greet at her studio located in a charming old town area a short drive from my home, its streets lined with pubs, wine bars, and coffee shops with delicious pastries. I liked the idea of meeting at a studio where I could play an acoustic piano. It sounded more enjoyable than leading an instructor to my cold basement where the view from the keyboard was an egress window, visited by the occasional field mouse or snake. Her space was cheerful with plenty of natural light and a black grand piano.

The meet and greet went as I expected. We chatted about my current practice, what I liked and disliked, and why I was seeking lessons. From a file cabinet, she pulled pieces of music similar in difficulty to what I told her I had been playing on the app. And I could not read any of them. She pulled easier pieces from the file cabinet, which I also could not read. She continued to pull easier and easier pieces, one after another, until we found something that I could read and play.

I could have viewed this as a humiliating experience, playing "Für Elise" on an app, unable to play it from sheet music and then regressing to "Yankee Doodle" and "Row, Row, Row Your Boat" on the acoustic piano. But my instructor remained cheerful, patient, and kind. I was surprised at how comfortable I felt, fumbling along. I took pictures of her books to order online, scheduled a lesson for the following month, and left her studio feeling hopeful. I reminded myself that I am an adult, with neither a deadline nor expectations. I was learning piano in my fifties to Foster Joy and Creativity, damn it!

The books arrived a week later, and I practiced throughout March, thirty to forty-five minutes daily, progressing halfway through the first book. Technically, my session with the instructor had only been a meet and greet. We had scheduled my first real lesson in one month—April Fool's Day. Yikes!

***

In March, I planned to begin a hot yoga trial when I returned from visiting my parents in California mid-month. But two days after I arrived home, a large snowstorm hit Colorado, making it questionable if I could make the drive to the classes, or if classes would be canceled altogether. Also, due to the snow, we scheduled a ski trip the following week, so it made more sense to postpone a hot yoga trial to later in March.

During our ski trip, I thought about how I was spending my time, and I was hesitant to add an additional physical activity to my list. Though I loved yoga—possibly more than any other form of exercise—planning around it proved an onerous task. Typically, I began preparing for a yoga class the day prior, drinking enough water to be adequately hydrated for a morning class, but stopping early enough prior to bed. The morning of, I planned my breakfast in both timing and quantity, to be neither too full and nauseous, nor too hungry and depleted. Bikram yoga classes took ninety minutes, and only studios in Boulder proper offered these classes. Allowing for driving, parking, and time to secure a good spot in the studio meant blocking two and a half hours and coordinating our car schedule with class times. I felt comfortable with this level of planning to hike a fourteener—arranging gear, building burritos, filling hydration packs, arriving at the trailhead prior to sunrise—but a similar effort applied to yoga classes felt unmanageable...and fussy. And lastly, a monthly yoga membership was twice the cost of swimming at the rec center, so justifying it financially meant attending classes at least three times per week.

Hot yoga was transcendent, no doubt, but swimming had somewhat filled that gap for me. I emerged from the pool light and calm, much as I did from yoga, and decided not to begin yoga in March. Maybe I had fulfilled Promoting Health and Wellness enough for the time being.

While searching for new recipes during the holidays, I found one for nutrition bars similar to GoMacro MacroBars, a convenient snack to maintain energy while active. Scott and I have eaten our way through a variety of nutrition bars over the decades. We ate the original PowerBars in the '90s, chocolate-dipped Kind Bars in the aughties, and we currently eat both RXBars and MacroBars. I seek a balance of natural, pronounceable ingredients, adequate protein, and low glycemic ingredients. And taste! They cannot taste ersatz or have a mealy texture. Nutrition bars, though compact and convenient, typically cost $3–4 each. I hoped to create a bar that would be less expensive and more nutritious. I love baking and had included this activity within the Fostering Joy and Creativity category, though these bars were technically raw. Baking minus the oven part!

I realized Scott and I mostly ate the bars while skiing, camping, and hiking, little of which we did in late March, during shoulder season in Colorado. Ski season neared its end, and hiking and camping season had not yet begun. I was mostly running and swimming, short-duration activities that did not require conveniently packaged food, so I decided to postpone creating the nutrition bars until later in the year.

***

According to Britannica.com, pit bulls are not a specific breed but rather a category of dogs, a term applied to breeds such as the Bull Terrier, American Staffordshire Terrier, and Staffordshire Bull Terrier. The American Kennel Club (AKC) does not recognize "pit bull" as a distinct breed. When I lived in California, I often saw pit bulls and avoided them, even crossing the street when walking our Labrador Retriever. To me, these dogs symbolized aggression, like the intimidating "Derek" portrayed so compellingly by Edward Norton in *American History X.*

My perspective shifted after moving to Colorado. Here, pit bulls with spike collars were not accessories for tough men in tank tops, but loving companions to my neighbors in sweats and Uggs, walking their dogs—named Boogie or Cookie—before work. Colorado pit bulls wore cheerful collars adorned with flowers or dancing Grateful Dead bears. While stopping to pet these affectionate dogs—eager for attention and butt scratches—I discovered their trademark smiles and gentle natures.

Their humans did not adopt them to look tough but adopted them because the dogs needed and deserved love.

Pit bulls face unique challenges. They comprise a disproportionately large percentage of shelter dogs due to overpopulation, a result of irresponsible breeding and a lack of neutering or spaying. There is a public perception that pit bulls are inherently more aggressive than other breeds, leading to breed-specific legislation (BSL) that bans or restricts certain breeds and further complicates their lives. Families unable to find housing that allows pit bulls often surrender their dogs to shelters.

During my years volunteering at an animal shelter, I grew to appreciate the personalities of these so-called pit bull breeds—affectionate, intelligent, and eager to please. Many puppies already knew basic commands like "sit," and every pit bull I walked was potty-trained. Inspired by their friendly smiles, I wanted to design a button (button-badge) for pit bull lovers to celebrate their charm and warmth.

Although I began designing the button, I did not finish the project in March. Knowing that spring and summer would bring plenty of outdoor activities, I decided to pause the project and revisit it during a colder month when indoor creative pursuits felt more fitting.

March Check-In

Take piano lessons ◯
Sign up for a hot yoga trial ◯
Make nutrition bars ◯
Design a pit bull button ◯

Q1 Retrospective

At the end of March, I reviewed my first three months of activities across four categories: Making the World a Better Place, Fostering Joy and Creativity, Promoting Health and Wellness, and Strengthening and Expanding Relationships. In the first three, I had made consistent progress, completing multiple activities in each. However, I had not completed anything specifically aimed at Strengthening and Expanding Relationships.

I did not feel socially disconnected. Our recent travels focused on deepening bonds with family and long-time friends, with hikes, local food, and cultural experiences serving as wonderful bonuses. I also attended a monthly neighborhood book club and scheduled quarterly lunches with a former colleague. But just as moving to new cities had taught me to make friends before I needed them, I didn't want to be months into retirement and then—*bam!*—suddenly feel isolated and lonely. I hoped that by joining activities I would build connections that would develop into local friendships.

I noticed, however, that activities designed to meet new people—though enjoyable—had not yet led to friendships. Volunteering, for example, was largely solitary as neither walking shelter dogs nor restocking ED supplies lent itself to sustained social connection. Similarly, while I enjoyed the camaraderie of my women's cycling group during events, rides, and coffee stops, the interactions remained confined to the group setting. Was I wrong to expect it to blossom into deeper friendships?

On reflection, I realized the issue lay in my allocation of activities. Many that I categorized under Strengthening and Expanding Relationships also belonged to other categories. Pickleball and yoga, while having social potential, primarily aligned with Promoting Health and Wellness. Joining a local habitat conservation group fell within Making the World a Better Place. None were solely focused on building new relationships or deepening existing relationships. That needed to change. I recognized that, to cultivate deeper, more meaningful connections, I needed to intentionally prioritize building and maintaining relationships.

Eight

April

- **Train for blue gravel**
- **Paint bedroom acrylics**
- **Begin landscape designs**
- **Make nutrition bars**
- **Take pickleball lessons**

Piano lessons had been on my list since February, but my first actual lesson was not until April 1. Throughout March, I practiced daily. My process had included scanning the song's QR code, watching and listening to a video of a professional, playing the song myself, and then revisiting the professional's version for reference. I practiced each song until I could perform it without errors. That first lesson turned out to be completely different from the meet and greet.

When I arrived at my lesson, my book bristled with orange Post-It notes marking the songs I had practiced. I played each song for my instructor, and she was thrilled with my progress! She explained that her typical first lesson involved reviewing songs with new students, but since I could already play them, her original plan went out the window. We played duets together, something I had never done before. Despite the simplicity of the songs, the experience was fun! For the first time, I read and played music. We smiled and laughed through the session.

"As musicians," she said, "it's our job to pay attention to the melody." Melody isn't just a sequence of notes; it is the part of the music we carry with us, the tune we recognize and hum long after the song ends. She encouraged me to play along with the professionals in the videos because, while I was hitting the right notes, sometimes the melody lost its shape. Paying attention to the melody—not just accuracy—felt as though it applied to more than a piano lesson.

My daily trips to the basement no longer felt like another item to check off my list. *I'm a person who plays an instrument*, I thought, marveling at the shift. While I would not call piano playing a passion—at least, not yet—it had started to bring me a level of joy.

Ensō and Sweet Spot of a Cold

By mid-April, I had made little progress on my activities for the month. We traveled the first week in April and returned home to cold, wet weather that resulted in canceled group rides. Bad for cycling, good for indoor creative projects.

Our California home had blank walls—a constant reminder of our indecision over which art to display. But in Colorado, we had embraced a more carpe diem mentality, deciding to make our space feel like home without waiting for perfection. "Don't let perfect be the enemy of done," we reminded ourselves.

During the pandemic, I painted three acrylic canvases with ensō designs—simple, incomplete circles meant to symbolize imperfection, the beauty of a moment, and emptiness. Intended as placeholders in our prior townhouse dining room until we found "real" art, their simplicity grew on us. They now hang above a desk in my office, too minimalist for the drama of our great room.

For our master bedroom, I had purchased three large blank canvases, intending to create something bold to cover the massive wall and hide the unsightly TV-ready outlets—we are not bedroom TV people. One of my Fostering Joy and Creativity activities for April was to finally bring those canvases to life and out of the basement. I thought they might be temporary like the ensŌs, but I have learned that temporary can sometimes surprise us with its staying power.

Wet weather gave me the excuse to dive into both my landscape designs and my painting project. For inspiration, I scrolled through my Pinterest boards, large, abstract pieces with blobby, soothing shapes in cool tones. On a brisk Wednesday after swimming, I queued up a few episodes of my favorite podcast, "This Jungian Life," pulled on my painting clothes over my regular layers (our basement can be downright arctic), and got to work.

Two hours later, I emerged with paint-smeared hands and a sense of accomplishment. The canvases were far from perfect—I mean, really far. I was not even sure they were done, but I left them to dry in the basement, giving myself time to decide if they might become more than just another "temporary" solution.

***

Within my cycling group, as in skiing, there are three levels—green, blue, and black. For the past three seasons, I had joined green rides, the easiest in terms of distance and speed. But by the end of last season, I joined two blue gravel rides and was comfortable with the faster pace and longer distance. I hoped to train to join more blue gravel rides as part of my Strengthening and Expanding Relationships and Promoting Health and Wellness categories.

But there would be no training in April. Likely due to our travel, I contracted a cold with symptoms that lasted ten days. Rarely ill or injured, I took the opportunity to binge award-winning artsy films too weird for anyone else to sit through, their surrealism enhanced by my feverish or tranquilized state. The downtime, not something I often allow myself while healthy, I spent on the sofa watching *Black Swan*, *Dream Scenario*, and *Poor Things*. It reminded me of a *New Yorker* cartoon, "The Sweet Spot of Flu," where a person lies on the sofa covered by a blanket. Two overhead bubbles capture the sentiment of being ill enough to watch TV guilt-free, but not so ill that watching TV is treacherous.

Lying on the sofa in the middle of the day to watch a movie—unless in the sweet spot of a cold—felt verboten, even in retirement. But the unplanned and rare stillness, though forced, gave me an opportunity to recharge. Regeneration came from doing nothing. I wondered, *Do I need to find more of that, more stillness, more…nothing?*

Yummy Tomatoes and Lekker Bars

During the pandemic, we had successfully grown tomatoes in containers on our Colorado townhouse patio and looked forward to expanding our efforts in this home. Nobody grows tomatoes to save money—homegrown tomatoes are entirely about the taste, worlds apart from grocery store tomatoes! I was thrilled to finally have a backyard spacious enough for a vegetable garden. Our house came with standard grass lawns in the front and back yards, easy to maintain, yet uninspiring. Lawns do little to support local ecosystems. Our goal was to eventually replace the grass with xeriscaping to reduce water usage, add a pollinator garden, and build raised garden beds for vegetables—squarely within the category of Making the World a Better Place.

A local organization plants pollinator gardens in the open space around our neighborhood. It is fun to spend a morning with neighbors in the dirt, weeding, digging, and planting. These 300-square-foot gardens of native plants establish quickly and require little water, resulting in small pollinator islands that create habitats for bees and butterflies. They also help preserve genetic diversity and resiliency in plant and insect populations. In our individual yards, we can create garden beds of native species, and then have it certified as a native habitat. I wanted to make one of the garden beds in our front yard part of the local pollinator district.

To visualize the transformation, I turned to the design software I had relied on for years: Chief Architect Home Designer. This tool, a simplified and more affordable version of the tool professionals use, allows for realistic 3D renderings of home interiors and exteriors. While designing can be complex and occasionally frustrating, I enjoy the creative challenge it provides. With April already in its fourth week, I began landscaping designs.

I started with a copy of the plot plan to establish dimensions, then measured the existing gravel, grass, and hardscape. Capturing the yard's exterior elevations was particularly challenging. Unlike interior designs where cabinets and walls anchor the space, working outdoors required creating terrain perimeters and contours to account for the yard's slopes, almost as if I were designing a miniature golf course. After plenty of trial and error, I managed to draft a basic rendering of our yard with its existing grass, gravel, and fences.

***

Understanding the imminence of warmer weather, I searched for the nutrition bar recipe I found over the holidays and purchased the ingredients, all of which I had used before, except brown rice syrup. I am not a huge fan of purchasing items for a single, specialized use, and my hope was that, after making the recipe with brown rice syrup, I could swap it for honey. The bars were simple to make, no-bake, with good flavor. The chocolate chips were noticeable but not overpowering. I could taste the almonds and brown rice syrup but, happily, not much of the protein powder. If you have tasted protein powder, you know how it can create a flavor black hole—its dry, bitter taste sucking the life out of everything else, a flavor vacuum that drags all moisture into its void.

I named them "Lekker Bars," as lekker translates to "delicious" or "tasty" in Dutch. The bars contained more fat than commercial

MacroBars with slightly fewer carbohydrates. Would they be filling enough to provide adequate energy without feeling like a lump in my stomach? Only time would tell how their sustainability would compare to commercial bars.

One of the women from book club mentioned that pickleball was especially social. Beyond pickleball's appeal to my social goals, I was also drawn to the pickleball clothing—cheerful tennis skirts and dresses in happy colors, not unlike the cycling kits that first caught my eye and inspired me to join a cycling club. I hoped that having played tennis in high school would make learning another racket sport easier.

As I reflected on my activities from January, February, and March, however, I realized pickleball would require a significant time commitment. With the improving April weather, I planned to return to cycling, which made my schedule even more full. I had already decided to drop hot yoga—an activity I knew I loved. Taking up pickleball, a complete unknown, felt impractical. I crossed it off my list, for good, without regret.

April Check-In

Train for blue gravel ○
Paint bedroom acrylics √
Begin landscape designs √
Make nutrition bars √
~~Take Pickleball Lessons~~

Nine

May

- **Train for blue gravel**
- **Practice clipping in**
- **Attend two low-stakes social events**
- **Complete three landscape designs**
- **Plant a vegetable garden**

May held great potential! The weather warmed, and Scott and I had no scheduled travel to detract from my planned activities. After shaking off a lingering cold, I felt grateful just to be moving again, returning to the water. While driving to the rec center to swim, I noticed a distinct surge of lightness—maybe even joy—that I described as a happiness spike. I wondered if not just doing my activities, but also writing about them, was a factor.

I am no stranger to navel-gazing; its technical term "omphaloskepsis." For years, in the same spot on our peacock blue sofa, my writing practice included interpreting the previous night's dreams and writing "Morning Pages," daily journals where I chronicled mundane parts of my days, worrisome or annoying conversations, successful recipes, astrology, and current obsessions. Morning Pages, so named in Julia Cameron's *The Artist's Way*, were a veritable mind Zamboni, clearing mental clutter and getting noise out of my head and onto the page.

Sometimes it became creative and even meaningful. It was just not...gratifying.

But writing about my retirement activities felt different. Knowing I would write about them forced me to examine each endeavor with a beginner's mind. Did I like it, or just the idea of it? Could I lose myself in it, or was it more about the outcome? Had I experienced the elusive state known as flow? In the past, my tendencies toward managing outcomes sometimes caused me to procrastinate doing something new or avoid it entirely, thinking I needed different weather, more research, or some arbitrary timeline like "when we return from Austin." Knowing I would write about both successes and failures had the opposite effect. If I learned anything from my twenties, it was that bad decisions make better stories. That knowledge imbued me with an audacity to just *do the thing* instead of waiting for conditions to be perfect. So, I jumped in.

I opened a new folder in Google Drive, titled it "Act II," and filled it with documents and spreadsheets. And once I chose writing, the creative guilt and angst I carried about not pursuing other creative projects quieted. I no longer had to debate every possibility. A watercolor painting–class invitation landed in my inbox, and I deleted it. A stray idea for a Substack essay, I captured in Notes and set aside, not allowing it to distract me. When a photo wall idea bubbled up on Pinterest, I pinned it and moved on. In limitation, I found freedom.

Freaked Out and Clipped In

After recovering from my April cold, I returned to cycling in May, gradually increasing both the speed and distance of my rides. I had my eye on a posted sixty-five-mile blue gravel ride, but since illness and weather had kept me from completing rides over forty miles, I decided to hold off and joined a green ride instead, a leisurely route of less than twenty miles. Its slow pace strengthened my resolve to move up to blue gravel rides.

Things were going smoothly—until mile eight, when my chain fell off due to a bent derailleur. I couldn't fix it on the spot, cutting my ride short just as I was hitting a good rhythm. Although I felt disappointed, the experience reminded me of the kindness and generosity of people on the trail. Two cyclists from my group stopped to help, one getting her gloves greasy trying to fix my chain, the other ensuring I had a plan to get home. Several solo cyclists also stopped to ask if I needed assistance. When my Uber driver arrived, he carefully loaded my dirty bike into his pristine car. I apologized profusely about the potential mess, but he waved it off, saying, "Don't worry about it." As he drove, he spoke about his love of the area and hiking, making for a pleasant ride.

Back at my car, I drove to a local bike repair shop. Even on a busy Saturday, the manager walked me and my bike to the back, where a technician fixed the derailleur in about ten minutes. When I asked how much I owed, the woman at the register smiled and said, "Don't worry about it." I drove home grateful and with a full heart.

The following week, I joined a blue gravel ride—thirty miles with a faster pace and typical elevation gain. As we gathered in the parking lot, I felt a mix of excitement and nerves. The women chatted about Left Hand Canyon, a single-track trail, not a gravel path though rolling hills. I didn't ride too many single tracks, and the thought of navigating a narrow, unmaintained path—with rocky terrain and ruts from erosion— made me a little anxious.

Once we started, I found the pace surprisingly comfortable. I had prepared well: hydrated, slightly caffeinated, and fueled with oatmeal— and the weather was perfect. I rode most of the way beside a woman with plenty of cycling experience. As we pedaled, she shared stories about living in different places, her love of camping, and her plans to spend the afternoon gardening.

About two-thirds into the ride, we stopped for a break while the leader explained what to expect on the single track. As we tackled it, I found myself spooked a couple of times and pulled off to the side to regroup. But each time, I hopped back on the trail, determined to keep going. The steep uphill portion challenged me the most, with loose gravel that forced me to dismount briefly. Still, I made it through most of the climb on my bike, and the sense of accomplishment upstaged every moment of effort.

At the end of the ride, my dirt tan began at my socks and extended past my knees. I was filthy, tired, and incredibly happy. I thanked both the ride leader and the woman with whom I had spent most of the ride chatting. It had been a positively good day—one that left me feeling strong, connected, and deeply satisfied. It was time for the next step: learning to clip in.

Clipping in—being physically tethered to anything outside myself—unnerved me. It took me right back to the single SCUBA lesson I abandoned in a resort pool, panicking at the idea of trusting equipment to breathe. My attachment style objected on principle.

I know I cannot progress without taking the leap, so I cross the Rubicon and text Scott.

"I'd like to work on clipping in."

Everything online described clipping in as "a secure connection between your shoes and your pedals," so it is difficult to explain my irrational fear. Is there loss of control when it takes two movements—instead of one—to get my foot from the pedal to the ground? Is it attachment to a thing outside of myself? Or is the panic of being locked in when I want an exit, a half-second delay between falling and saving myself, stretching into something bigger?

Scott ordered the cleats—along with his and hers "F*ck This, Let's Ride" socks—which arrived in early May and promptly sat untouched for two weeks. When he asked if I planned to use them (the cleats, not the socks), I half-heartedly watched a five-minute YouTube tutorial, marked my shoes with a Sharpie, and stalled. The next day, Scott texted.

"Shoes are ready to be tested. Don't get sweaty palms."

The next morning, I practiced in the garage, clipping in and out of one pedal. After a few tries, it felt manageable, so I mapped a flat, familiar trail for my first ride. For two miles, I clipped in one foot at a time, staying close to home in case disaster struck. Eventually, I clipped in both feet, cautiously unclipping near pedestrians, dogs—anything remotely unpredictable.

Ten miles later, I had survived, but I didn't feel triumphant. The ride felt heavy, as if clipping in had stolen the joy of cycling. I had hyperfocused on the next turn, hill, or gravel patch, constantly anticipating when to unclip.

On another ride, days later, I stopped on a trail blocked by a passing train. While resting to eat a Lekker Bar, I watched prairie dogs chirp and scurry. Some lounged along the path in shallow indentations they made in the fine, sun-warmed gravel, refusing to budge as if to say, "It's my summer too." The sight filled me with both delight and sadness. Prairie dogs are a keystone species in Colorado, vital to the ecosystem. Like the central stone of an arch, without them, the ecosystem collapses. Though not yet endangered, their habitats are vanishing, bulldozed for shopping centers and apartment buildings.

The sight reminded me of the way I felt at the summit in Glacier National Park, appreciation immediately followed by dread, one moment captivated by prairie dog coterie antics, and the next pondering ecological collapse. Was it guilt, carrying knowledge of our precarious interdependence while at the same time anthropomorphizing their behaviors, allowing myself to be entertained? Or was it the realization of how insignificant I was, powerless to save their habitat? A permeable barrier separated the gift of reverential delight from the cost of its disappearance, but to ride by and miss it entirely seemed worse. Maybe, like l'appel du vide, the prairie dog–triggered existential dread was life-affirming and signaled my capacity for awe and wonder.

After the break (and existential mini crisis), I debated whether to ride home or tackle a hill toward Boulder, and I chose the hill. While many cyclists relish the downhill, I find it unsettling—unpredictable winds, the loss of control. But climbing? That grounds me. It is rhythmic and meditative, one pedal stroke at a time. I remained clipped in for the entire climb, only unclipping briefly for a sharp turn at the top. By the time I reached home, I had ridden twenty miles—less than my usual distance, but enough for that day. It was neither fun nor easy, but I knew progress had begun.

Irish Goodbyes, French Exits, and Aussie Tim-Tams

Drawing on my Q1 assessment that my Expanding and Strengthening Relationships category was lacking, I set an intention in May to participate in two low-stakes social events: a volunteer appreciation dinner for the pet shelter and our neighborhood garage sale. I considered an event "low-stakes" if the invitation was communicated via an app or group email and allowed for an Irish Goodbye or French Exit.

At the dinner, a woman approached the table where I sat with two others and asked if she could join us. I invited her to sit down, introduced myself and the others, and asked her questions to start a conversation. She answered my questions politely and then looked at her plate or glanced around the room.

I assume that people who make the effort to shower and dress, drive to an event, and then sit at a table for eight have at least some expectations of social engagement. Conversations, by definition, are an oral exchange. So, I find it frustrating when someone answers questions but does not ask any in return. Why must I do all the heavy lifting? It makes me want to say, "This is the part where you ask me a question—I am not interviewing you for a magazine."

I call these people ZQs—Zero Questioners. Whether socially awkward, distracted, or self-involved, ZQs often signal disinterest in others.

Behavior researcher Alison Wood Brooks, author of *Talk: The Science of Conversation and the Art of Being Ourselves*, advises that conversations progress from small talk toward something more meaningful not as a social obligation, but as a doorway to connection.

Few of us relish talking about the weather or what we are doing over a three-day weekend, but what is the alternative? Remaining silent? Not making new friends and being alone? Trauma dumping?

I felt disappointed in my table. The woman who joined us—the ZQ—continued to stare at her plate. Meanwhile, the couple across from me represented the opposite extreme. A woman loudly rattled off facts about shelter leashing policies while her husband sat in mute compliance. I laughed to myself thinking, "This is why they work with animals."

But I had to check myself—the people at my table were not working a checklist for Strengthening and Expanding Relationships. Community is not about perfect chemistry or sparkling conversation; it is about shared purpose. Whatever our social strengths or blind spots, we kept showing up for the animals. And that, ultimately, made me glad to be at the table. And there were cupcakes.

The second event was our neighborhood garage sale, which I had missed the year prior, thinking I should organize my art supplies in the basement instead. Initially, I didn't think we had much to sell—some clothing and a few housewares we planned to donate. But as we began gathering items in the garage the day before, our pile grew larger than expected, spilling into the dining room. By the time we had finished, we had more than enough to justify setting up shop.

Two hours before the sale, we moved everything to the driveway. I hung the clothes on my ballet barre, which gave the display a surprisingly professional look. A table held smaller items—electronics, planter pots, and glassware—while an outdoor rug showcased shoes, throw blankets, and pillow covers.

Throughout the day, neighborhood kids stopped by to chat and pet Remi, a friend's dog we were watching. Neighbors came to say hello, and I had conversations with people who had driven into the neighborhood specifically for the sale. My precocious ten-year-old neighbor joined me for a while, and we discussed my pricing strategy, why certain items like shoes attracted attention and others did not.

Though the day required several hours of organizing, selling, and interacting with buyers, I enjoyed it—despite only making $100. It was not entirely about the money but about participating in the community and finding new homes for items I no longer needed, without the hassle of transporting them elsewhere. By the afternoon, both Remi and I were exhausted, but I felt glad I had chosen to participate.

***

In April, I had begun designing landscapes with the intention of completing three designs in May. By the second week of May, I had completed the exterior elevations—the slopes, retaining walls, and areas of gravel and grass—creating an approximation of our existing yard.

For the front yard, I added garden beds and a steppingstone path leading from the sidewalk to our front walk. In the backyard, I envisioned trees along the fence line to block traffic noise when wind blew from the east, raised vegetable garden beds at the back, and beds extending beyond the existing flagstone pavers. Once I finalized the first plan, I showed Scott a dollhouse view of the property with my additions.

"Wow," Scott said. "This is ambitious."

I walked him through the features, starting with the trees along the east fence line.

"Planting trees there is risky," he said. "It might block our neighbors' view, and it could even be an HOA issue. Plus, trees are expensive, and there's no guarantee they'll survive the winter."

He pointed to the backyard's southeast corner. "Because of the slope, we wouldn't even see them from the house."

Scott had a point. We agreed that planting trees, at least in that spot, was not the best use of our time or resources—especially since our primary goal was to focus on summer planting.

Next, we discussed the two garden beds in the front yard. These seemed manageable since they had existing irrigation. We could remove the large gravel, outline the garden beds, and add soil, plants, and mulch. The steppingstones were more complicated, however, as they would require digging up the grass and potentially disrupting irrigation lines. From past projects, we knew that opening up surfaces often led to unexpected challenges. The steppingstones, we decided, would have to wait. Turning to the raised beds in the backyard, I had proposed placing them along the fence line, which borders open space.

"I'm not sure about that," Scott said. "What if the wildlife eats everything? Plus, if the beds are closer to the house, we could water them with a hose. Setting up irrigation back there could be tricky. And what about the grass—would we dig it up, kill it, or mow around it?"

His concerns were valid. Our yard often hosted rabbits, snakes, and field mice, while coyotes howled at night. Neighbors had also spotted raccoons and opossums. Planting vegetables so close to their territory seemed unwise. We decided to place the raised beds near the house in the side yard, even if it meant removing gravel.

I also planned to fill six large pots with flowers and herbs before summer. By the end of our discussion, I felt satisfied. Scott's input helped me concentrate on what we could realistically accomplish in the three weeks before summer, reducing my sense of overwhelm. Again, I found relief in choosing less. We ordered raised bed containers, and Scott began researching the cost and logistics of gravel removal.

I updated the plan to include front yard garden beds, raised beds in the side yard, three pots on the front walk, and three pots in the backyard. Rather than creating two additional landscape designs in May, I realized the first design was adequate for our immediate needs.

The last two weeks in May, Scott and I spent researching soil mixes, assembling the raised beds, and placing them in the side yard after removing the gravel. In Colorado, we often get a big snowstorm Mother's Day weekend, so typically, nobody plants before then. Scott rented a trailer to haul bulk soil, and with help from our ten-year-old neighbor, we spent the morning with our hands in the dirt, filling the planters and blending in compost, peat moss, and potting soil. After we filled the raised beds with dirt and compost, I planted a combination of plants and seeds—three cherry tomato plants, three sweet pepper plants, two rows of radish seeds, and three rows of Delicata squash seeds. It was a rewarding way to start the day, capped off sharing cups of Earl Grey tea and our favorite Aussie treat—Tim Tams.

The nutrition bars I created in April—or Lekker Bars, as I named them—were too fatty, so once we ate the first batch, I tried again. I swapped the ground almonds for rolled oats and cut the bars in larger slices, which made them more substantial. The updated recipe turned out to be just right—replacing almonds with oats increased the carbohydrates and reduced the fat, providing better energy without sacrificing flavor. I dubbed this recipe "Joyful Almond" and froze them, wrapped them in compostable wax paper for our rides and hikes. With a basic recipe that worked nutritionally, I felt excited to attempt new flavors. My mind was already racing with ideas, starting with a tahini, date, and honey combination I would call "Hot Date with My Honey."

May Check-In

Train for blue gravel √
Practice clipping in √
Attend two low-stakes social events √
Complete ~~three~~ one landscape design √
Plant a vegetable garden √

With the warmer weather, cycling had ramped up, and my rides stretched to four hours, three times a week. Hiking season would soon begin as the snow melted in the high country. The completed landscape design had brought new tasks—clearing gravel, filling planters, and tending to the front and backyard pots and garden beds. Beyond the initial labor, I would water daily and weed weekly. And I was writing about all of it! Had I taken on too much?

That night, a dream echoed my growing concerns—but not in the way I expected. It was not the usual dream, where I realize a final exam is in three days for a class I haven't attended all semester. This dream felt more like a trial of the self. I was shown that I longed for creativity, freedom, and truth, but remained entangled in the need to appear acceptable—performing subtle acts of self-correction to maintain the status quo. Lucid and aware in the dream, I tried to fly to prove to myself I was dreaming, but someone held my legs.

There is a tension between what I know I am capable of and what I allow myself to step into, a subtle but persistent fear of my own power. This emerges when I push myself physically or express myself creatively in a way that feels bold—as if some part of me believes that wanting too much or stretching beyond the expected will invite not just criticism but possibly punishment. I hold back, self-correct, or downplay my desires as a form of preemptive protection. Still, the longing remains.

In the past, I might have told myself that my activities—creative pursuits, wellness routines, the effort of building friendships—were enough, and that I should simply be grateful for the time and space to enjoy them. I might have even convinced myself to step back from writing, telling myself it took too much time or that I didn't know where it would lead. But in the dream, I recognized the familiar shadows—fear of criticism from those who linger safely on the sidelines, fear of unsettling others' expectations of me, fear of disrupting appearances. I reminded myself—those characters were only projections. This time, I would not shrink. I would trust myself.

Ten

June

- **Visit two farmers markets**
- **Make summer cookbook recipes**
- **Buy fresh flowers**
- **Wear summer clothes**
- **Watch more movies**
- **Eat dinner outside**

Though I romanticized summers as having a languid quality, aside from a twenty-minute nap, a lot of GSD (get sh*t done) happened between breakfast and dinner. To remedy that, though I would continue to write, I decided June activities should not add to my current lift. I wanted to step out of the categories I had created and allow myself to appreciate summer. Et pourquoi pas?

Sitting in the backyard on a sunny afternoon, under the umbrella enjoying the breeze, I created a list of summer recollections.

- Whoosh of a Coleman lantern, trilling blackbirds, and chirping crickets.
- Juicy, sweet Palisades peaches, watermelon sliced into triangles, warm berry cobblers with vanilla bean ice cream, and icy rosé.

- Scents of SEA & SKI, charcoal briquettes, chlorine on my skin, barbecues, roasting marshmallows, campfires, and herbaceous air after summer rain showers.

- Spaghetti straps, the rush of A/C walking by automatic doors, summer produce at farmers markets, breezy dresses in saturated hues, and licking an ice cream cone while walking.

- Dozing on a blanket under spring green oak tree canopies; jumping through sprinklers with my sister and drinking from the hose; dinners of corn-on-the-cob, barbecued chicken, fruit salad, and blackberry cobbler on my parents' deck.

Fresh Produce, Fresh Flowers, Fresh Threads

I lovingly refer to farmers markets as "the farket." When I lived in Long Beach, I went every Sunday and enjoyed speaking with vendors who directed me toward the level of ripeness suitable for my recipe timeline. I felt eager to try unfamiliar produce and vendors' cooking suggestions. Though the produce is sometimes more costly than grocery store produce, its flavor and quality are always superior.

I visited a small local farket on a weekday and felt disappointed with its lack of produce stands, specifically summer fruits and vegetables. Most of the stands sold artisan goods like honey, bread and muffins, handmade soap, or other locally made consumables—perfect for gifts, but not what I was looking for. I resolved to visit farkets next month in neighboring towns to find one that suited my needs.

Like many people, I have several cookbooks full of recipes I have never made. Though many of the recipes looked and sounded delicious, I never made them—too complex or too heavy with animal products. Some required something I did not own like a special pan or a mandolin (hello, finger guillotine). I tend toward minimalism with kitchen gadgets, though more recently I had reminded myself to acquire tools I needed for the job. It seemed silly to ignore delicious-looking recipes because I did not have a simple tart pan. In the category Promoting Health and Wellness, I aimed to make one new recipe every week for the month of June.

I took full advantage of the bounty of summer produce throughout June. I made a watermelon, blueberry, and mint fruit salad, and served it with wheat berries and Scott's barbecued chili lime shrimp. I roasted sriracha lime sweet potatoes that we ate with a zucchini ribbon salad, adding fresh herbs harvested from the backyard pots and toasted pine nuts. Scott barbecued halibut to accompany my green apple, arugula, and roasted hazelnut salad. An easy cold soba noodle salad with shredded chicken, crisp vegetables, and chopped cashews was a perfect hot summer dinner.

These delicious recipes incorporated variations of ripe fruits and fresh vegetables we already enjoyed. Preparing the natural, succulent summer ingredients not only enhanced my appreciation of summer, but it also sprung us from our dinner rut.

I enjoyed June! I stuck with my intentions to make the month feel like summer without adding to my existing commitments. I noticed "Pickling vegetables" on my spreadsheet, and though I had not planned to pickle in June, we had carrots, radishes, and onions on hand. I tackled the easy pickling recipe and relished the results. Pickled vegetables—especially the onions—elevated our salads and barbecued Mediterranean eggplant wraps, plus the pink liquid created by the red onions and radishes made me smile whenever I opened the fridge.

I cared for several plants throughout our home, but in June, I wanted to revel in the small indulgence of fresh flowers. Not only do flowers look beautiful by adding color to a home, but they also make me appreciate summer and its ephemeral joys. And I am not the only one.

According to the American Society for Horticultural Science, a study of appendectomy patients showed that patients in hospital rooms with plants and flowers required significantly fewer postoperative analgesics, showed more positive physiological responses evidenced by lower systolic blood pressure and heart rate, lower ratings of pain, anxiety, and fatigue, and more positive feelings and higher satisfaction about their rooms when compared with patients in the control group.

I bought fresh flowers twice in June, yellow tulips and pink Gerber daisies. Tulips have always been my favorite flower with their elegantly rounded shape and bright hues, and the cheery look and long vase life of Gerber daisies puts a smile on my face. Seeing flowers on the dining table each day brought a small but noticeable lift, a reminder of summer's brightness. Their colors and simple beauty mirrored the lightness of the season, making ordinary moments feel a bit more joyful.

***

Just as I have always loved tulips, I have also loved fashion since playing dress-up as a little girl. I grew up in the foothills of Northern California where people dressed casually, so "Don't you look nice" felt more like an accusation than a compliment. I looked forward to Halloween, when our mother sewed Halloween costumes, and I became a mouse, lion, Flamenco dancer, or a '50s girl in a poodle skirt. As an adult, I showed up to parties as Cruella in a black and white wig or as Tippi Hedren from *The Birds*, fake crows stuck in my hair and pinned to my shoulders. Kate Spade said, "Playing dress up begins at age five and never really ends."

I wished I had more opportunities to dress up as an adult, but living in Colorado and working from home provided few opportunities beyond leggings and hoodies. Not that I didn't try. On the pet wall in my former downtown Denver office hung a picture of me holding my colleague's Cairn Terrier, Lucy, the two of us twinning in matching faux fur collars. I wore a thrifted faux Chinchilla coat to a fall garden party and promptly returned it—and its mob wife vibes—to the car. For a volunteer dinner, I layered a vintage silk Chinese robe over a white-ribbed tank and distressed jeans.

While running errands and driving to the grocery store, I typically resorted to athleisure—Lululemon tights, slides, and a zipped jacket. To the recreation center over my swimsuit, I wore an Adidas tracksuit for its easy on/off qualities. But for the summer, I wanted to wear stylish and unique pieces daily, not just on special occasions. Dresses are easy to move around in, look "put together," and are chicer and more flattering than shorts, especially when paired with bright sandals and a summer bag. There is a quiet defiance in wearing a splashy, patterned dress in Boulder, a town known for its earthy-crunchy aesthetic.

My two long sleeve, patterned summer midi dresses are not for the faint of heart—they draw significant attention. Whoever said women become invisible after forty-five has never worn Farm Rio dresses. No wonder their site says, "Get ready to dress in happiness!" Whenever I wear these dresses, I receive compliments in the stores I visit and while walking down the street. Women have stopped their cars, rolled down their windows, and shouted, "Your dress is beautiful!" A store employee stopped in the parking lot and clapped his hands in applause. "Ma'am, that dress is exquisite!" People who work in design have stopped to take pictures of the fabric. It is both flattering and entertaining that a summer dress can elicit this much enthusiasm.

Athleisure attire made me want to rush off to accomplish the next item on a to-do list—not at all leisurely. But summer dresses made me feel engaged with and curious about my surroundings, instilling a desire to linger. The small act of wearing a summer dress helped cultivate and embody the languid feel of summer I aimed for, almost like a vacation.

Barbenheimer and Cantilever Umbrellas

2024 was the rare year that I watched many of the Academy Award–nominated films. Sometimes I have never even heard of the films, let alone watched them, but several of the nominated films interested me:

Oppenheimer, *The Holdovers*, and *Barbie*. Coincidentally, my parents were watching the Oscars while I visited them in the spring.

"So, you have seen quite a few of the films," my mom said.

"I guess I have," I said, surprised at myself.

I did not see myself as a person who often appreciated Academy Award–nominated films. Remember *The Artist* from 2011? On the rare occasion that we went to the theater, we watched action franchises too big for the Academy—*Mission: Impossible* or *James Bond*. My rainy weekend noirish cinematic pics did well at festivals but were typically too small for Best Picture nominations. Though I do not have network television to watch the Oscars, I recognize their cultural significance, while bemoaning their lack of diversity.

But walking through my parents' family room as Best Picture was announced, I felt excited—not simply from awareness of a film's title and logline but engagement with the stories. Sure, I had enjoyed the films for their entertainment value, but I also appreciated their thought-provoking themes. I felt a level of connection toward the character experiences and narratives. Bearing witness to the craftsmanship of cinema had brought me joy, and I wanted more.

Though Scott or I often suggested watching a movie over the weekend, we would return habitually in the evenings to the series we were already watching. Summer seemed like a good opportunity to watch more movies, so I set an intention to watch one movie per week.

Was this in the category of Fostering Joy and Creativity or Et Pourquoi Pas? I wasn't sure I cared.

But this called for a spreadsheet!

I created one tab to track television series and another for movies, then added Oscar-nominated films to the list to watch over the summer. *May December, Maestro, American Fiction, Nyad, The Zone of Interest*—each weekend, instead of our usual series, we watched a movie.

Some of these movies we would not have chosen on our own, but that made the experience richer. It expanded our entertainment choices beyond the usual three-letter-agency espionage thrillers, immersing us in different eras, places, and perspectives. And isn't that why humans make art in the first place—to tell stories in ways they have not been told before?

***

Beyond introducing more movies into our weekends, I also hoped to shake up our evening routine and dine outside under the cantilever umbrella in our backyard at least once a week. Simple in theory—complex in execution. Colorado weather is famously unpredictable. As the saying goes, "If you don't like the weather, wait fifteen minutes." We can experience all four seasons in a single day, making al fresco dining a gamble. Too much wind? The umbrella stays closed. Too hot? Forget it. And the first week of June didn't help my cause—it brought temperatures soaring into the nineties, keeping us indoors.

By late June, we had not eaten a single dinner outside. We had managed lunch out there once, but dinner? Never. It was always something: the heat, a poorly timed gust of wind, or meals ill-suited for our patio setup—a pair of oversized lounge chairs and a small side table. I loved the idea of a serene evening with a gentle breeze, carrying plates of food to a shaded backyard table with sweating glasses of icy rosé. But reality was less accommodating. Colorado, for all its beauty, rarely offers temperate, still evenings.

One afternoon, while sketching under the cantilever umbrella, a sudden gust of wind proved my point. It lifted the massive umbrella off the ground, toppling it onto the grass and tearing the fabric at the seam. No wonder people choose posts and sails over umbrellas in Colorado.

June Check-In

Visit ~~two~~ a farmers market √
Make summer cookbook recipes √
Pickle vegetables (bonus) √
Buy fresh flowers √
Wear summer clothes √
Watch more movies √
Eat dinner outside ○

Mid-Year Review

The purpose of a mid-year review is to align goals, review progress, and get feedback to ensure the second half of the year stays on track. On the last day of June, I held one for myself. I looked back at six months of leisure activities—swimming, planting a garden, cycling, piano—all part of my experiment to treat retirement like a project worth documenting. I wanted a life that reflected my values, a retirement lived with intention. But toward the end of May, intention had started to feel like performance. Was I shaping a life of meaning or curating one that only appeared meaningful?

I was not bored. Clearly, I had plenty of activities to fill my time, and I liked writing about them. Along the way, I met new people and made friends. I didn't feel as though I had lost my identity—but maybe it was because I was managing my retirement like it was another project. And in a way, it was.

When people asked about my work, I said, "I retired in December from managing software projects."

Then came the inevitable follow-up: "Do you miss it?"

My answer was an immediate and enthusiastic "Nope." What exactly would I miss? Well, maybe the healthcare.

I had restarted blood donations in January and continued to donate blood every eight weeks. Composting had become a daily habit, and we dragged half a barrel to the curb for pick up every two weeks. Between curbside recycling, the plastic bags I dropped at the grocery for recycling, and composting, we had little actual trash going to landfills. I stuck with the washable hankies I had begun using in January to replace facial tissues. Except for creating a pollinator garden, everything in this category of my intentions spreadsheet had been completed. I could not say for sure that the world was better, but my corner of it was!

Most of my activities to Foster Joy and Creativity were one-offs. Some creative projects like painting acrylics (still in the basement) and designing landscapes provided joy in the moment. Others like practicing feng shui and creating Lekker Bars offered recurring bursts of joy when I walked by the tidy, intentionally arranged shelves in my office or when I ate Lekker Bars on rides and shared the recipes with my cycling friends.

The most significant activity I had undertaken to Foster Joy and Creativity was learning piano, and I continued to play thirty minutes daily and attend monthly lessons. Did that foster joy? I did not always look forward to daily practice, but I liked the idea of progressing toward a creative effort, and I felt satisfaction when I mastered a song. I reminded myself to think in layers, that if I continued to play year after year, then by the age of seventy-three, I would have twenty years of experience.

"What is your piano endgame?" Scott asked me one afternoon when I returned from a lesson.

"Two things," I said. "I want to select a piece of music and then learn to play it. Also, I want a sustaining hobby to build upon and enjoy for decades, something sedentary to appreciate when I am no longer able to hike thirteeners and fourteeners or ride my gravel bike."

In retirement parlance, the phases when time and age slow our abilities and activities are known as "slow-go" and "no-go" years, in contrast to the early "go-go" years of retirement when we travel and enjoy active pursuits. Go-go, slow-go, and no-go years are typically mentioned in the context of saving for "go-go" year expenditures, a subject that Scott had been reading about and sharing with me for years. When I considered my own future, I realized that piano could be more than just a hobby—it could be a companion that carried me through every phase, giving me both challenge and solace when my world eventually became smaller.

Maintaining our garden mostly brought me joy. I snipped potted herbs regularly, which lent freshness and interest to our salads, and I excitedly picked ripe tomatoes. While watering the raised beds, I examined sprouts from the radishes and delicata squash and watched the miniature peppers grow larger each day. I pruned dead stalks or leaves and inspected discoloration on leaves and branches. Around the beds, I performed small chores like weeding the gravel walk and then stood back to look at my well-kept path. I believed the plants, growing on their own timetable in the rhythm of the season, had something to teach me.

I had been knocking wellness and fitness out of the park, especially the fitness portion! Lap swimming, I continued three times per week, 2,000 yards each swim. In May, I clipped in and trained for blue gravel rides, and in June, I joined them, comfortably maintaining the pace.

One Saturday, I left the house early and rode north, planning for a long ride of fifty miles on a familiar trail to further practice riding while clipped in. The previous week's temperatures had been warm, melting snow in the high country, which caused Boulder Creek to overflow, so I waded through creek water nearly up to my knees. The weather was warm, so I did not mind having wet shoes and socks.

While stopped to look at my Google Maps with one foot clipped in, I tipped over. Though unhurt, I did get dirty. I stopped at a nearby cafe, sipped a decaf cortado while sitting under an umbrella, and ate my newest Lekker Bar creation of tahini, honey, and dates, "Hot Date with My Honey."

When I hopped on my bike, however, the chain began to catch, and I realized that, again, my derailleur was bent, and the bike was unrideable, so once again, I called an UberXL. Three days later, I discovered a giant bruise on my left bum cheek that resembled the ever-present storm on the planet Jupiter.

With my bike repaired, I joined a forty-mile blue gravel ride the following weekend with my cycling group. I clipped in and unclipped when we came to stops as everyone else did, keeping pace. As we rode, I participated in conversations, allowing my mind to wander away from my feet, appreciating the beautiful scenery and warm weather. I felt strong and happy, my Lekker Bar providing the energy I needed. At the end of the forty-mile ride, I had remained clipped in for about 80 percent—a commendable endeavor.

I shared with a ride leader that I was new to clipping in, and she reminded me to not be tempted to unclip on steep hills with gravel or sand.

"The wheels want to turn," she said. "Shift to the granny gear and pedal."

When I told her about my trepidation riding downhill, she suggested I loosen my grip on the handlebars, relax my upper body to absorb shock, and center my bodyweight over the seat. It helped.

I felt particularly happy one Saturday when I rode solo on a fairly steep segment of a trail in dry, sandy gravel and didn't panic and unclip. I remembered her words and told myself, "Pedal, pedal, pedal!" and made it to the top of the hill where it leveled out. A runner commented on my speed.

"I can't believe how fast you did that," she said.

I felt seen! Sometimes I was trapped in my little world, worried about falling and failing, and then a stranger offered encouraging words. To a more experienced rider, the segment may have been unmemorable, but to me, it felt like proof of progress!

As the weather grew warmer, I left the house earlier, each day becoming less aware of being clipped into pedals. I became more vocal, ringing my bell as I approached runners on the trail, even when I was sure they were aware of my presence. I rang my bell as I approached tunnels, bridges, and blind curves, warning anybody with whom I could possibly collide. My perceived danger of being physically attached to the bike had made me a safer cyclist. What once felt like a vulnerability had transformed into a heightened sense of awareness, turning caution into confidence with every ride.

Something I was not doing to Promote Health and Wellness was performing monthly breast exams. Though I did not have a family history of breast cancer, I knew this was not a free pass. I added monthly self-exams to my wellness and fitness list, and in the spirit of "Save the Boobies," I added an entry to my private calendar: "Monthly (.)(.)".

***

In building community, I struggled. Adult friendships are notoriously difficult—not just to cultivate but also to maintain. Rosie Spinks, in her Substack essay "The Friendship Problem," described modern friendship as "nearly admin." Even getting someone to commit to coffee can feel impossible—people cancel, they don't follow up, or they disappear into the abyss of "We should get together!" I get it. Why go to the effort of meeting a friend who loves rom-coms when I can sink into something deliciously dark and twisty on Netflix?

Spinks attributes this flakiness to our obsession with "friction-free" living. We have grown accustomed to convenience—Amazon Prime, contact-free food delivery, streaming entertainment, and text messages that require no real-time conversation. She quotes Esther Perel, who speaks about loneliness on a podcast:

> Modern loneliness masks itself as hyper connectivity. And so, people have easily 1,000 virtual friends, but no one they can ask to feed their cat. That loneliness, which is really a depletion of the social capital, is extremely powerful.

Social media reflects this social atrophy. Tweets lament the burden of putting on pants, memes celebrate introversion (though conflating it with social anxiety), and Facebook posts romanticize low-maintenance friendships—no fancy dinner parties, just impromptu trips to Target.

I did not believe I had socially atrophied—if anything, the pandemic made me more aware of my social needs. But after moving to Colorado in 2017, I found myself without many friends I could ask to feed a proverbial cat. (More of a dog person here.)

Spinks pinpoints the problem: "The career-mindedness, the self-optimization, the adventures, the travel, the trying to survive in desirable places to live which become comically expensive to do so—all of it has left us very tired."

Check, check, check, check, and check. I had done all of it. It was not just a side effect of moving to a new state—it was a pattern. I did an abysmal job of maintaining friendships from high school and college. But in my fifties, I had begun to view friendships differently. I rekindled a friendship with a high school friend, and now, we text regularly. She still lives in my hometown in the foothills of Northern California, as do my parents. I enjoy seeing my old world through her eyes when I visit— we meet for lunch or walk together and laugh about the resurging popularity of '80s bands.

I revived a friendship with my roommate from my twenties, visiting her in her family's new town, wine-tasting and laughing about our lives in LA in the '90s. I found relief in these friendships from so many years ago, before I knew well enough to be judicious and appear "put to-gether." And I maintained friendships from my longtime home of Long Beach, finding comfort in the continuity. Knowing this reassures me that I am not a sociopath.

In Colorado, I wanted to form local friendships and expand my circle of proverbial cat feeders. During my neighborhood's community garage sale, I had casual, easy conversations with neighbors and felt more con-nected to my community because of it. When I joined my cycling group's rides, I found myself talking to women close to my age. Two were planning for retirement, and one was a project manager—instantly, we had common ground.

I thought about where I could make more friends—a neighborhood clothing swap, a monthly walking group or movie club. I mentioned this idea to Scott.

"You seem to like organizing fun stuff, but does it translate into ac-tual friendships?" he asked.

He had a point. I liked planning events, and I liked the initial excite-ment of a new group. But maybe I needed to focus on deepening the friendships I had already started rather than chasing new ones. Accept-ing myself as I am—not someone who effortlessly maintains lifelong friendships—I asked myself, *How can I expand and strengthen my re-lationships in a way that feels authentic, enjoyable, and realistic?*

I wanted friendships where I could send a simple text. "Want to grab coffee?" or "Up for a morning gravel ride?" I decided to start with ex-isting connections—my cycling group, my neighbors, and my book club. Beginning in July, I would make two deliberate efforts to meet with someone locally. Then, I realized nothing stopped me from starting now. Why wait for July? I had phone numbers, and I could just reach out. So, I did. I texted one of the women from book club, and we made a date to walk to coffee.

We met at the trail the following week, walked to coffee at a local café, and had great conversations! We chatted about travel, our plans for retirement, and the pros and cons of our parents living in California. Throughout the summer, we continued to meet for walks, joined by her sweet, energetic doodle, who greeted me with kisses. And as we walked, she didn't just ask, "How are you?" and then launch into her own stories. She asked pointed questions. I answered, she built on it, and we kept going.

My topics in conversation, I admit, occasionally veer toward the random and arcane. I notice zeitgeists or behaviors in the milieu, or I relate life's random and mundane details to a conundrum. I once referred to my heavily patched jeans as "Ship of Theseus denim." I hurl my wry observational grenades, non-sequiturs designed to destabilize diatribes and glimpse others' inner worlds, an escape hatch from self-referential stories I have heard a hundred times. I might ask, "How do you feel about clowns?" Scott referred to this as doing my "shock and awe." It is goofy and eccentric—I know this about myself.

But this felt like a real conversation—engaging, reciprocal, present. Questions, answers, follow-ups—simple yet rare. The real attention and subtle curiosity made all the difference to me. She remembered what I said on our last walk and asked me about it. During these walks, neither of us were relegated to the role of friend-apist. It was not performative, and there were no humblebrags. I felt listened to. And because she listened—really listened—I let myself say it out loud, "I am writing a book."

Eleven

July

- **Visit two farkets**
- **Plan two friend dates**
- **Attend a low-stakes social event**
- **Make four camping recipes**

On the heels of our May garage sale, throughout June, Scott and I made further progress selling items on Facebook Marketplace and donating items we no longer needed. We then focused our attention on our list—another spreadsheet—of house projects we initially cited as to-dos when we moved into our house two years prior. Repainting our fence was imminent.

Mid-month, Scott and I would travel to the mountains for five days to ride in an organized gravel cycling event, and my sister and niece were scheduled to visit for three nights toward the end of the month, which overlapped with dog-sitting. In addition, I wanted to build on the lessons I had learned about forming friendships as an adult somewhat new to my neighborhood and continue the summer vibes I had cultivated in June. All of this made July feel ripe with possibility.

Farkets and Friend Dates

I still wanted to visit farkets with produce stands selling summer fruits and vegetables. The first Saturday in July, I drove to the farket in a neighboring town, way too excited about the close, easy parking. I walked along the main street, happy to see all the produce stands lining it—stands selling fresh herbs, mushrooms, fruit, tomatoes, cucumbers, salad greens, and vegetables. It mirrored what I had envisioned for the farket! Shaved ice, handmade jewelry, and cinnamon bun stands lined a street running perpendicular to the main street, a delineation I appreciated.

With the heirloom tomatoes I brought home, I made a tomato and basil open face sandwich on seed bread I had baked the evening prior. Well, it was intended to be an open face sandwich, but the toast broke when I removed it from the toaster, so I ended up with a tomato and basil torn bread salad with olive oil, sea salt, and freshly ground pepper. Still delicious!

On another too-hot Saturday, realizing it was the last weekend in July, I rushed out of the house an hour before the farket closed and purchased a cantaloupe, yellow cherry tomatoes, small Persian cucumbers, peaches, plums, and shishito peppers. I also bought a hand-embroidered pillow cover and a handmade wool ombré handbag as Christmas gifts—local items that caught my eye as opposed to shopping on Amazon and department stores in December. Leaving with my arms full of summer's bounty and thoughtfully chosen gifts, I felt the tranquil satisfaction of fulfilling my intention—two farkets, two experiences, and a month well spent.

I had set an intention to plan two friend dates for July. I met a long-time friend for breakfast on the Fourth of July weekend, and seeing each other was long overdue. Despite our twenty-five-year friendship, we have been more couple friends than girlfriends, rarely connecting without our husbands. My friend travels frequently for work, and her husband's profession follows a traditional Monday through Friday schedule, so when we see each other, typically all four of us gather on weekends, barbecuing, camping, or meeting for dinner. It was great to catch up, undisturbed by cooking, tending to campfires, or ordering drinks and dinner courses.

My second friend date I scheduled in advance. We are former colleagues and worked in the same Denver office prior to Covid. It is entertaining to me when I meet socially with project managers—talk about no drama llamas! With many people, I face indecision, a negotiation of days and times, or lengthy exchanges of ancillary information concerning prospective meeting times. With project managers, there is none of that. One person provides a window of availability, e.g., "Busy until after the 13th and then open after that," and the other affirms an available date, "Okay, let's do Saturday the 20th." There is no waffling. A meeting time is agreed upon, and typically one of us sends a confirmation text the day prior. Nobody gets lost, and we show up early.

Typically, my friend and I plan something cultural like visiting museums followed by lunch. Though we had intended to see an outdoor exhibit in southern Denver, by mid-July, we were both weary from hundred-degree temperatures. We opted for air-con alternatives: a rom-com movie followed by a cocktail. Though different from our usual outings, the laughter and easy conversation reminded me that the company mattered more than the itinerary.

My intention to "Attend a low-stakes social event" was simple—go to one new social gathering each month with familiar faces, like neighbors, fellow volunteers, and other local women. I hoped it would help solidify existing connections and possibly launch new friendships. An event that caught my eye was a monthly social night at a local consignment store. Normally, I skip evening events—I am a morning person to the core. But this event was held monthly and immediately followed my volunteer shift in the ED, so I figured I could swing it.

But of course, July's timing was less than ideal. The event fell the night before Scott and I left for a cycling trip in the mountains. We had a long list of to-dos—packing, prepping food for the road, making sure not to forget anything important (like the bikes). After the hustle, the last thing I wanted was to socialize. I craved a quiet dinner on the sofa with Scott and our cozy prestige TV escape. I passed on the event and snuggled in for an evening of relaxation. And you know what? It was exactly what I needed.

Though we had not scheduled our camping trip until early September, I had received a vegetarian camping cookbook for Christmas. I enjoyed cooking new recipes and wanted to try them prior to camping, so I added this within the category Fostering Joy and Creativity. But I did not make a single camping recipe. I had no desire to fire up the oven or stove with temperatures in the nineties—I could not imagine eating one-pot meals in warm bowls. I moved this activity to August, which made more sense due to our two-week camping trip planned in September.

July Check-In

Visit two farmers markets √
Plan two friend dates √
Attend a low-stakes social event ○
Make four camping recipes ○

I filled July with literal garden-variety activities, with temperatures often in the nineties. After my morning ride, swim, run, or dog walk, I grabbed my wide-brimmed hiking hat and the gardening gloves Scott bought me at the start of summer and headed to the backyard. Weeding became a daily ritual as they seemed to pop up overnight through the pea gravel walkway leading to the garden beds. Watering took only about twenty minutes each day, but time seemed to slow while doing so. Without distractions like podcasts or texts, I found myself in the moment. While standing over the plants, I observed water pooling around their bases and closely examined each one—flower blooms, leaves with holes, budding fruit, and changes in the soil. If tomato branches jutted outside their cages, I carefully guided them back in and rested them upon the next closest layer of galvanized steel. When stalks began to sag under the weight of ripening peppers, I propped them up with small sticks and rocks. I had begun harvesting sweet cherry tomatoes—about a dozen a week.

As July dragged on, the intense heat made everything feel sluggish and lethargic. I felt disappointed when my sister and niece canceled their July visit due to illness. Our summer book club selections did not excite me, though I recognized that I had not suggested many books myself. Even cycling became a source of indifference—our group rides typically met at nine o'clock, far too late in the sweltering heat. By then, I had already been on the trail for over two and a half hours!

Volunteering at the hospital's ED on Wednesdays had also lost its appeal. Supply chain issues affected my ability to stock medical supplies and blanket warmers—not that anyone asked for warm blankets in July. Though I still felt grateful for the time to give back, everything I once looked forward to felt like a chore. But just as the relentless heat would eventually break, I reminded myself that other things—illness, supply chains, my own sense of stagnation—were also cyclical. I could either wait for change or take small steps to help myself. Embracing the ebb and flow of seasons, I focused on what I could adjust to rekindle joy.

I browsed the best books lists of the *New York Times* and the *New Yorker* and uploaded titles to my book club's page for "Books we want to read." I shifted my dog shelter volunteer shift to cooler mornings, a relief for both me and the dogs, who greeted me with grateful enthusiasm. I called my sister to plan a fall visit with her family in Portland. Enthusiasm, like cooler days, would return in time.

Twelve

August

- **Join two blue gravel rides**
- **Attend the gravel clinic**

In August, the house projects Scott and I had taken on began to tighten around us—driving across Denver in the heat; meeting contractors; collecting estimates for doors, windows, and tile, and closet designs. We approached projects differently—he preferred to gather pricing information for multiple projects upfront, while I liked to prioritize details for projects we would tackle soon. Gathering quotes for projects we would not begin for six months felt pointless—prices, lead times, and availability would all change by then. I looked at an initial design for the master closet and thought about my socks that currently shared a drawer with my workout clothing. I had made the arrangement work, but it was not ideal. I began to lose interest.

The heat and ennui from July followed me into August. When I looked at my list of activities, I felt disinterested in them all. Though I knew it was not entirely true, it felt like I had no room for anything new. The activities became too reminiscent of work, when my days felt like Tetris games, frantically flipping falling shapes, completing horizontal lines that vanished immediately. And the shapes kept falling. By the time I finished exercising, gardening, and practicing piano, half the day had finished.

Three months into summer, the garden offered a mix of progress and disappointment. The radishes grew in small and too spicy, a result of the summer heat. Brown spots and blossom-end rot speckled the peppers, probably a sign of calcium deficiency. Though they were still edible, the rot made them unappealing. Cartoonish tomato hornworms stripped the tops of my tomato plants, and I spent afternoons plucking them off, tossing them into the field behind our house. After my neighbor told me she had chased a rabbit from a bed three feet off the ground, I surrounded the delicata squash with chicken wire. The pests and brown spots slowly replaced my early excitement with a creeping sense of futility.

Despite the setbacks, I continued harvesting tiny cherry tomatoes, delicious on their own or tossed into salads. Beneath the large squash leaves, I noticed delicata squash growing and felt a thrill each time I found a new blossom. The potted herbs remained untouched by pests, and I added basil and oregano to salads and sauces and rosemary to bread and roasted vegetables.

Eventually, the sense of overwhelm told me I needed to scale back. I reminded myself that this experiment was not about productivity or proving anything—it was meant to bring joy to this season of life. August did not need more activities, especially with travel planned around Scott's cycling events—one long weekend in Copper Mountain and another in Taos, New Mexico. I decided to focus on my current activities, adding only gravel rides that would take up a morning or afternoon— time I would have spent cycling solo anyway.

Kitty Litter and NozKons

I prefer gravel cycling to road cycling because I don't like sharing the road with cars. Gravel bike paths and country roads weave through open spaces and beautiful countryside, offering the adventure of cycling without the technical demands of mountain biking. To build my confidence, I signed up for a gravel clinic to learn techniques for handling tight corners, riding in loose gravel, and positioning myself for safer descents.

The clinic, hosted by a local company associated with my cycling group, was scheduled for midday. As the date approached, the forecast predicted temperatures in the nineties. While waiting in the parking lot, I struck up conversations with other women in the group. One of them lived in my neighborhood, so we exchanged numbers, hoping to plan a morning ride together. Another woman wore a small leather patch on her nose, clipped to her sunglasses. She explained that the "NozKon" helped protect her sun-damaged skin. After having cancerous spots removed from her nose years ago, she swore by it. I made a mental note to order one when I returned home.

As we continued to wait, the heat intensified. Feeling slightly nauseated, I debated heading home, but instead, I squeezed into the limited shade, trying to stay cool until we started. Once our group finally set out, we rode along the LoBo Trail—a familiar route connecting Boulder and Longmont—before reaching the "kitty litter" gravel where we would practice.

The instructor covered key techniques for maintaining speed on loose gravel and taking corners with control. I learned how to pedal and brake simultaneously and discovered that it was perfectly fine to let my tires drift off the trail, as they would still grip the dirt or weeds beyond the gravel. She taught us how to adjust our body position for better balance in turns. The tips were invaluable, and despite the brutal heat, I enjoyed the learning and camaraderie.

Two days later, I met up with my newly discovered neighbor for a short morning gravel ride—a great way to get exercise and enjoy some conversation.

I did not fully realize how much I had absorbed from my training until later that month at my cycling group's summer party. One of the women asked me about the clinic, and as I began explaining what I had learned, descriptions of the skills and techniques came back effortlessly. Another woman, overhearing me, walked up and asked, "Oh, do you teach the clinic?"

I laughed. "Oh, my gosh, no! That was my first gravel clinic. But clearly, it was worth it—I still remember everything a month later!"

Looking back, it amazed me how much I had gained from a single clinic. Not only did I ride away with more skill and confidence, but I also met a new friend—and ordered a NozKon!

Before hitting my stride in a physical activity, I have always needed a significant warm-up. On my high school tennis team, in singles, I typically lost the first three games before rallying to either win or at least make it a close match. The same pattern plays out in hiking: I start off slow, trailing behind Scott as we ascend, only to pick up the pace midway, practically running down the mountain by the end. Cycling is no different for me. I begin conservatively, hanging toward the back of the pack, then gradually work my way forward as I warm up.

After spending the summer clipped in training for blue gravel rides, by August, I covered longer distances at a faster pace. I joined a relatively fast thirty-mile blue gravel ride through the country roads of Niwot and Gunbarrel, looping around the reservoirs and ponds in Lagerman Preserve. I had to push hard at the start to keep up, surprised at the brisk pace. But it was a beautiful day, and by the time I rolled back to my car at noon with my bike, tired and satisfied with my water bottles and calves covered in fine dry dust, I felt accomplished.

The next August ride extended nearly forty miles, starting in Boulder and weaving through Louisville and Superior, with a stop at a charming café in Lafayette. I always enjoy mid-ride coffee breaks—they offer a chance to get to know the other women better, even if the stops are brief. On this ride, I debuted my newly purchased NozKon. It was not remotely stylish, and when I posted a picture to my socials while wearing it, someone compared me to Hannibal Lecter! Still, vanity took a backseat to function—if I could keep up with blue gravel rides, I could certainly handle looking a little ridiculous. Besides, our riding kits were cute enough to balance it out…or so I told myself.

August Check-In

Join two blue gravel rides √
Attend the gravel clinic √

Thirteen

September

- **Find a Jungian therapist**
- **Plan meals for camping trip**
- **Try the cold plunge pool**
- **Schedule a bike fitting**

In August, due to burnout, I had taken a break from thinking about and categorizing my activities—all two of them. Even writing had become a chore, forced and monotonous, so I took a break from that as well. Burnout comes from doing too much, demanding too much of oneself, and trying to hold it all at once. I never notice I am heading toward it until I am already in its throes. It's like bonking on a long hike—my glycogen runs out, and my legs turn to lead. My head spins, and I feel an emptiness nothing can fill fast enough. By then, it is hard to recover. On the trails, I know how to protect myself: I eat early, refuel, and measure the miles. But when it comes to writing, managing house projects, or hosting during the holidays, there are no built-in guardrails. I let myself get too low.

I call it The Dryness, which has nothing to do with perimenopause, PMS, depression, or Mercury in retrograde. The Dryness follows burnout, and the muse up and leaves for an unknown period of time.

Sometimes she leaves during home construction, visitors, or travel. With the muse away, I cannot remember my dreams. Books, articles, and podcasts become dull and uninspiring—everything is pointless and stupid. Spotify background jazz seems to play a single song the entire day. People repeat stories about the most mundane topics. Inanity. It feels as though we have been eating the same five dinners for months. My attempts at creativity are futile, every effort a shadow of what once flowed easily. I cannot text the muse and say, "Time to come home."

So, I perform activities that typically cause her to want to return home. I spend time outdoors without headphones. I meditate with a greater intention of emptiness. I drink more water, light a candle in the early mornings, and open the slider to hear the birds. I listen to moody playlists while preparing seasonal dishes or tidying a corner of my home. I pile juicy tangerines into the carved wooden bowl on our dining room table, or I buy a bouquet of tulips. I pin inspirational quotes to remind myself that, "The first draft is just you telling yourself the story."

And then, one night, I awake from a dream and know that the muse has returned home.

I had been considering reaching out to a therapist—specifically, a Jungian therapist—in the category of Fostering Joy and Creativity. I did not feel depressed, anxious, or in crisis. On the contrary, I could not remember feeling happier than I had this year. But after listening to the brilliant podcast "This Jungian Life," where the hosts offered rich interpretations of listener dreams, I thought my own dreams might be a source of untapped potential.

In one episode, podcast host Joseph shared the story of a client suffering from writer's block who—after a few therapy sessions—experienced a creative breakthrough that unlocked the flow of words. I wondered if working with a Jungian therapist could have the same effect on me. Vivid and detailed, my dreams often played out as intricate narratives with recurring animus characters—sometimes even lucid. Surely, the decade's worth of subconscious material in my dream journals could fuel the novel I had been thinking about writing.

Using the online *Psychology Today* directory, I searched for a Jungian therapist who offered in-person sessions. Finding a therapist—especially since the pandemic—had already become a chore. Finding a *Jungian* therapist was even trickier. And finding one who saw clients in person? Nearly impossible.

But not quite.

In traditional talk therapy over the years, I shared with my therapists my difficulties related to my super-commutes, challenges surrounding colleagues, and ambivalence toward motherhood. Talk therapy provided tools to manage immediate concerns and laid the foundation for handling similar challenges in the future. There is a quote I love, though I can't seem to find its origin: "People in therapy are often in therapy to deal with the people in their lives who won't go to therapy."

My new Jungian therapist and I met, and from the start, we dove into the colorful, recurring characters of my dreams. Though I did not immediately begin writing the great American novel, I felt an instant connection. My therapist and I spoke a language unshared with anyone prior. In each session, she left me with a new understanding.

For a creative person, Jungian therapy—with its focus on archetypal themes and dream tapestry—connected me to my soul. It allowed me to see, for example, not just why being productive was not always productive, but also my reasons for needing to be useful in the first place. Jungian therapy didn't just give me insights into the nature of my creativity; it allowed me to embrace the urge to create without a constant need to justify it.

All the Gear, No Idea (with a Posh British Accent)

Scott and I learned years ago, while camping in America's Switzerland—Ouray, Colorado—that cooking full meals from scratch at a campsite is both exhausting and impractical. After a long day of hiking—often in unpredictable weather—having to prepare an entire meal from start to finish can quickly drain the joy from an otherwise enjoyable day. Over time, we have refined our approach to cooking one-pot meals at home, freezing them, and simply reheating them on a propane stove at camp as we leisurely review pictures from our hike and sip whiskey.

In the two weeks leading up to our ten-day September camping trip, I cooked and froze four one-pot entrees—beer and bean chili, spiced chickpea and rotisserie chicken biryani, red lentil curry, and kitchen sink veggie burgers. Kitchen sink veggie burgers contain a mix of remaining lentils, beans, grains, and nuts from the cupboard, formed into a patty, grilled, and served on a pretzel bun with all the fixings.

Each dish provided dinner for two nights, plus enough leftovers to wrap in tortillas for burritos to take on the hiking trail. To give ourselves a break from cooking and cleanup and to support the local economy, we also planned a couple of meals at locally owned restaurants. And, because camping calls for a little indulgence, I baked a batch of chocolate chip cookies.

The one-pot meals were a success! My mom used to say, "Camping makes everything taste better." Whether we sat at a picnic table, watching squirrels leap from tree to tree, or tucked ourselves under the tent's eve, gazing out over a lake, every bite felt richer, every meal more satisfying.

Another lesson we have learned from camping: Hot springs are a game-changer. After a long, steep hike, there is nothing like sinking into warm, mineral-rich water to ease the aches in my legs and the tension in my shoulders—especially when the soak is followed by dinner out instead of campsite cooking. On our most recent trip, we discovered the stunning Durango Hot Springs Resort and Spa. Nestled into the hillside, towering pines lined the beautifully landscaped pools, offering a seamless blend of nature and luxury. We found the facilities clean and modern, and unlike most hot springs, this one let us sip a glass of wine as we soaked gazing at red cliffs against a green forest backdrop.

I loved one feature especially: the cold plunge pool, hovering at a bracing fifty degrees. Situated next to a hundred-degree pool, it was easy—and exhilarating—to shift from warm to cold. The icy plunge invigorated us. Later, it thrilled me to discover that my local recreation center had installed one too—though theirs aimed for a biting forty-four degrees.

While swimming at the rec center, I struck up a conversation with a woman rehabbing a broken foot. She told me she had built up to eight minutes and swore it changed everything—inflammation, sleep, mood. Encouraged, I set a modest goal—two minutes—and surprised myself by staying for three. After the first forty-five seconds, the sting dulled into a strange calm. Each day, I pushed a little further until I hit six minutes. The experience left me feeling energized—almost euphoric— like a strong cup of coffee but with an added boost of clarity and a touch of chatty enthusiasm. It became a regular challenge, a test of resilience that left me not just revitalized but oddly addicted to the rush of pushing my limits.

A British idiom goes like this: "All the gear, no idea." It pokes fun at someone decked out with expensive equipment but lacking the skill to match—enthusiasm colliding with inexperience. That has never been my problem. If anything, I veer the other way, self-handicapping by denying myself adequate tools or resources. I purchase gear below my ability level—or avoid buying it altogether. Before purchasing my gravel bike, I rode a "garage-sale bike" along trails in yoga pants, trainers, and a turquoise helmet decorated with cartoon skulls. I pedaled thirty miles before I finally allowed myself proper cycling shorts with a chamois, or padded crotch. I used this behavior as a form of self-protection—if I failed, I could blame my lack of equipment instead of my lack of ability.

But that wasn't it—I was already doing the activities, just with unsuitable gear. I often excused it as minimalism, but underneath brewed something deeper: a question of identity and worthiness. I believed "real" practitioners deserved proper tools, and I was not yet one of them. I carried a kind of deferred deservingness, as if I had to prove commitment or competence before earning the right to show up outfitted and belong.

When I resumed swimming in February, I ordered two basic pairs of goggles online—both under twenty dollars, both with decent reviews—intending to return the one I liked least. Neither won a permanent place in my routine. They leaked, fogged up mid-lap, and left deep red indentations around my eyes that lingered for hours—goggle eyes.

In a Facebook group "Did You Swim Today?" I came across a thread about custom-fit goggles. One swimmer said they changed everything for him—no leaks, no fog, no raccoon eyes. I felt intrigued. At $80, they cost four times what I paid for my cheaper goggles, but I swam three times a week. If they worked, the cost would be worth it.

Custom goggles are designed to fit the exact contours of your face, reducing the suction that causes goggle marks and discomfort. I placed an order online and downloaded the company's app, which walked me through a face scan using my iPhone camera. The process was only mildly awkward: I needed my reading glasses to see the instructions, then had to take them off to complete the scan—a small comedy of middle-aged tech navigation. I appreciated that the company gave me the option to delete my scan afterward. The idea of my facial data floating around on a random server unsettled me. I pictured a *Mission: Impossible* scenario: my face used to infiltrate high-security vaults.

The goggles arrived about a week later. I have a small face, and at first, the lenses kept falling away from the nose bridge when I tried to put them on. Fortunately, the kit included several interchangeable nose pieces tucked into the case. After some trial and error, I found a combination that worked, and as promised, the goggles did not leak. The carrying case served as a welcome bonus—sturdy, easy to spot in my swim bag, and helpful for drying the goggles between swims.

About a month in, though, the lenses began to fog. I reached out to customer service, who responded promptly and sent a mini bottle of anti-fog spray. They also recommended a DIY solution: a mix of baby shampoo and water in a small spray bottle. Surprisingly, it worked. Now, between lap sets, I give the lenses a quick spritz and enjoy clear, fog-free, leak-proof swimming—finally.

Since purchasing my gravel bike three summers ago, Scott had been suggesting I get a proper fitting to ensure it was ergonomically sound. I procrastinated, knowing the fit would change once I clipped in. But purchasing custom swim goggles had taught me that suitable equipment that fit me properly was not indulgent; it made the activity comfortable enough to enjoy, rather than endure. When the pain in my right arm became too much to ignore, I scheduled an appointment. Surely, this fell under Promoting Health and Wellness.

After reviewing prices and recommendations from my cycling group, I booked a fitting at the Boulder shop where I originally purchased my bike. I opted for the basic two-hour session at $150—reasonable for a first fitting.

The technician was professional, kind, and incredibly knowledgeable. Using various tools, he measured my sit bones and foot arches, had me ride my bike on a trainer while he observed my form, and guided me through different positions to assess alignment. In addition to adjusting my seat height and handlebars, he recommended a more supportive seat with extra cushioning and insoles for my cycling shoes to improve my pedal alignment. I couldn't have been more satisfied! It served as a reminder that well-being often meant listening to my body, seeking the advice of an expert, and then implementing their suggestions.

Afterward, I rode a short six-mile loop, and everything felt great. But the real test came the next day—a thirty-five-mile blue gravel ride. Fortunately, the adjustments made all the difference: The bike felt smooth and comfortable, and the nagging pain in my arm...well...I hoped that would soon leave.

September Check-In

Find a Jungian therapist √
Plan meals for camping trip √
Try the cold plunge pool √
Schedule a bike fitting √

Q3 Retrospective

My overall approach to summer—savoring and appreciating its offerings—allowed me to feel creative and experience joy, as did my daily ritual of gardening. Our gravel race in Steamboat Springs was a day of pure fun—well-supported, challenging, and achingly beautiful. We loved the quaint downtown, delicious restaurants, independent shops, and local breweries, along with its cooler mountain temperatures.

But once we returned home, July's relentless heat in the nineties turned previously joyful activities into draining efforts. I continued walking shelter dogs, stocking ED supplies, donating blood, composting, and recycling plastic bags—small efforts to Make the World a

Better Place—but at times, those activities felt futile when the planet itself burned. Wildfires filled the air with smoke, obscuring the Rockies.

Still, I felt grateful to no longer be sitting at a desk and instead riding my bike past lakes and wildflower-filled pastures, planning one-pot camping meals, and soaking in bracingly cold plunge pools. I was in the best shape of my life—even my hair seemed healthier than in my twenties.

We had been invited to a surprise birthday party for a former colleague. It was fun and silly to jump from behind a wall and scream, "Happy Birthday!" We laughed about the logistics of planning a surprise party, and I caught up with colleagues over hard cider. And there was cake.

But while I found joy, others around me struggled—grappling with anxiety, job insecurity, or illness. So many feared November's election. I felt as though I could not fully share my gratitude and happiness with anyone but Scott, and that isolation weighed on me. It reminded me of how I felt during Covid. When others were burdened with job loss, childcare, illness, and mental health struggles, I found solace in the simplicity of life at home. The imperative to do everything—fitness, work, entertainment—within our own walls removed an onus that had sometimes felt crushing. Home felt cozy and restful, and I cherished the extra time with Scott.

I shared these reflections during a hike with Scott, at first describing my feeling as something akin to survivor's guilt. He reminded me that, yes, I was fortunate, and my circumstances had not resulted from luck alone—I had deliberately shaped this life. I revised my description of my feeling, calling it humble gratitude.

At the same time, I recognized that those in a slump, even temporarily, deserved compassion and empathy. But I refused to waste that energy on the chorus of complaints from Substack and Facebook, where outrage or ennui often seemed performative rather than personal. I unsubscribed from authors and groups who—rather than taking the next right step—appeared to dwell in helplessness and self-pity. While I chose to focus my energy on positive actions and compassion, I also knew that cultivating peace and progress required the strength to distance myself from negativity—both for my own well-being and to maintain a sense of clarity and perspective.

Fourteen

October

- **Make four fall recipes**
- **Visit Ya Ya Farms**
- **Sign up for a hot yoga trial**
- **Practice longer mediations**

The raised gardens that provided both learning experiences and a sense of pride in summer were winding down. One pepper plant turned out to be a variety of chili too hot for me, so I left ripe chilis on my neighbor's front porch for pickling. Our prolific tomato plants would continue to fruit until the first freeze. I harvested a dozen or so delicata squash, roasting them for salads before the vines withered under whitefly infestation. Next spring, I would plant basil and marigolds alongside the tomatoes and squash to naturally repel whiteflies, a suggestion from the women in my book club. With cooler temperatures, I no longer watered daily—a welcome relief. And just as my runs or swims often feel stronger after a short hiatus, a much-needed break from new activities in August and September reinvigorated me.

Sometime around September, about the same time temperatures begin to cool and the leaves change, the light turns different, having almost a pink hue when the sun is lower on the horizon and casts longer shadows. I do not always remember I look forward to it, but when I notice its glow, I always feel delighted. It ignites my excitement for all things autumn, my favorite season. I love the onset of cooler weather, the weight of a heavy blanket at night, and cycling on brisk mornings. "Back-to-school" fashions provide the perfect excuse to wear hats and scarves, and I especially love cooking fall recipes.

Colorado shoulder seasons can be unpredictable—summer and winter conditions often collide in a single afternoon. But this year, September and October delivered spectacular weather. We enjoyed an extended Indian Summer with cool mornings, mild afternoons in the sixties and seventies, and vibrant fall foliage. Unlike past years, when strong winds stripped the trees bare too soon, golden and red leaves lingered until Halloween.

Soup in a Samsonite and the Dirty Ya Ya

Though I originally hoped to make four new fall recipes in my category Fostering Joy and Creativity, traveling and hosting family made this unrealistic. I reminded myself that I could use my fall recipes to savor the season, not check off a to-do list, so I revisited some favorites.

In the early aughties—just before 9/11 reshaped airport security and banned liquids in carry-ons—Scott and I flew to the Bay Area for Thanksgiving at my cousin's house. I brought along a homemade apple-butternut squash soup. Once cooled and puréed, I funneled it into gallon-sized Ziploc bags, sucked the air out with a straw, and stacked the flat pouches neatly into a vintage hard-sided Samsonite train case. It is unthinkable now, traveling with homemade soup as luggage!

My family felt skeptical. Most of them had never heard of butternut squash, and its vivid orange hue stood out like a renegade on an otherwise beige Thanksgiving table. For decades, my family had cooked from a cemented menu: stuffing, mashed potatoes, turkey, the infamous green bean casserole, sweet potatoes with marshmallows, and store-bought dinner rolls. My mom, aunt, and cousin cooked what my grandmother once had, almost as a ritual. New dishes rarely appeared. But I had always been the eccentric cousin, so it made a certain sense that a mysterious orange soup would arrive in my suitcase.

To my surprise, the soup was a hit. It looked elegant served in my cousin's china, the amber liquid gleaming against delicate porcelain. Even my uncle, the family jokester—who once made us laugh by sketching cartoonish middle fingers in the condensation on fogged-up windows—offered his approval. It reminded him of the sweet potato pie his childhood neighbors used to make, he said, and suggested we add it to the official lineup.

On a cool fall afternoon in October, I made this recipe, served with homemade raisin pecan bread and a green salad. Scott and I delighted in our first fall soup, accompanied by warm, crusty bread and butter, while watching one of our favorite British series, *Slow Horses*.

A seasonal staple in our kitchen is pumpkin bread. Yes—more bread! I rotate between two quick bread recipes: one adapted from Mark Bittman's "Quick Whole Wheat Molasses Bread" and the other from Angela Liddon's blog *Oh She Glows*. I have tested all of Bittman's suggested variations and even invented a few of my own—my favorite is swapping molasses for honey, which gives the loaf a brighter, more floral sweetness.

I bake a loaf about every week and a half, most of it eaten by Scott during his long cycling rides. For years, homemade bread with almond butter and honey has served as our go-to fuel—for rides, hikes, and road trips alike. We buy organic almond butter made from nothing but roasted almonds—no sugar, no corn syrup, and never palm oil. Our honey comes from a former colleague who keeps beehives on his Denver rooftop. Each November, I send him the same message—"It's that time of year again"—and place my annual order. I keep enough to last the year and set aside a few jars as holiday gifts.

On Sundays, we have breakfast for dinner—roasted potatoes topped with poached eggs. Having a set Sunday meal helped stave off Sunday Scaries before retirement and now adds a comforting predictability to the end of the weekend. For fall, I swapped our usual roasted baby potatoes for sliced parsnips and yams. Parsnips, with their sweet, nutty flavor, roast beautifully with olive oil, freshly ground salt, and pepper.

Tempeh is a plant-based protein made from fermented soybeans. The fermentation process gives tempeh a firmer, more meat-like texture and may help our bodies to digest it. This recipe was unplanned. I googled "fall tempeh marinade" and found a simple four-ingredient recipe—whole grain mustard, maple syrup, tamari, and olive oil. It was easy and delicious! I marinated the tempeh for a couple of hours and then baked it for thirty minutes. I tossed the warm tempeh into a salad of power greens, ripe pears, chopped pistachios, dried figs, and roasted parsnips and yams from the night before. Scott declared it the best salad ever! With these four recipes, fall had officially arrived in our kitchen.

Ya Ya Farms is a local orchard and farm that hosts apple-picking events, farm-to-table dinners, and weddings. Its country store sells apple butter, jams, and cider, making it a favorite stop for my cycling group's annual ride to Hygiene, Colorado. In gravel riding, it is common to preface a route's name with "dirty," because that is what we are at the end of the ride. As the route to the orchard runs along gravel roads, we call it "The Dirty Ya Ya." We browse the store, enjoy fresh apple cider donuts, feed the donkeys, and take plenty of pictures.

Since biking limits what we can carry, I always return later to purchase jams and apple butters as holiday gifts. It is a way to support local farms while giving friends and family something delicious, local, and consumable—avoiding unnecessary "stuff" accumulation. This year, I picked up pear gin, strawberry lavender, and cherry jams, along with apple blackberry sauce.

Driving along country roads on a crisp fall morning to return to this farm felt like more than just a simple errand; it carried a sense of both community and continuity. Just as I had the year before, I wandered through the barn, scanning the store shelves with curiosity, eager to see which sauces and preserves this year's harvest yielded. Filling my basket, surrounded by the warmth of tradition and the abundance of fall, I felt deeply grateful to reside in Colorado, where simple joys like this were woven into everyday life. I did not stop to think if this aligned with my category for Fostering Joy and Creativity, but it certainly brought me joy. I knew that gifting the preserves and sauces would bring others joy as well.

Seeking Stillness, Finding Pirates

The Bikram yoga classes I had planned for February and then March never happened, but I had good reason to think I could join a week-long trial in October. With cooler weather tapering off my cycling routine, I finally had time for classes. However, I was still nursing elbow pain, lateral epicondylitis, in my right arm—an overuse injury likely caused by swimming and cycling.

Seeing my cycling buddies on my socials, in matching kits against the backdrop of October's golden leaves and sunny skies, was tough. Even more frustrating was spending mornings on a kickboard in the pool, trying to find a position that did not strain my neck. Though kicking rested my arm, it made me slow and uninspired, leaving the meditative state that lap swimming usually provided just out of reach.

I had hoped to start a yoga trial, but the studio near my home offered vinyasa rather than Bikram. Given my injury, I doubted sun salutations would be any easier on my elbow than swimming or cycling. I iced my elbow each morning, securing a bag of frozen peas to my forearm with an Ace bandage. Ultimately, I had to wait for my arm to heal before giving yoga another try.

I felt as though I had stumbled upon a kind of sweet spot and noticed a pattern emerging, something that wove through each quarter. It reminded me of the classic time-management analogy with rocks, pebbles, and sand—if you want it to fit in the jar, start with the rocks. If you put the sand in first, there is not enough room for everything else.

Swimming, learning piano, and clipping in were my rocks—challenging, growth-oriented, and satisfying. When I focused on a rock, I felt momentum, like my life moved forward in a measurable way. They were a source of pride, shaping the person I was becoming in this new phase, offering glimpses of my new identity. Pebbles were my mid-level commitments—activities that needed planning, habit-stacking, or some coordination like social gatherings, composting, blood donations. Not all of them brought me joy in the moment, but each single act built upon itself, offering a sense of meaning that deepened over time or grounded me in the community.

And then, there was the sand, pursuits I could dive into on a whim, like trying a new Lekker Bar recipe, dabbling in acrylic painting, or taking a cold plunge. Sometimes I simply checked them off the list; other times, they made me playful or felt oddly rewarding. Visiting a farm on a crisp fall morning offered joy in real-time. But these activities fell away first when energy ran low, especially those in the category Et Pourquoi Pas. But what if there was another category, one that time-management techniques, largely gathered from the corporate world, didn't talk about? What about emptiness? In retirement, maybe my jar didn't need to include everything. Maybe there should be space.

In January, I had struggled to incorporate longer meditations into my routine—I either forgot to meditate during the day or found myself too distracted after dinner by my gurgling stomach. But in October, I set a clear intention of three sessions per week, each lasting twenty to thirty minutes.

The urgency for getting on the trails early because "we're burning daylight" dissipated with hot weather. People always complained about dark mornings as we neared the fall time change, but I didn't mind them. I found darkness soothing, as though I had the world to myself while everyone slept. I felt relieved that the weather was turning, a freeze inevitable, and as melancholic as it sounded, my plants would wither and die after the frost. My days felt less crowded, leaving space for stillness. So, after exercising, I made a habit of heading to our basement office to meditate. The basement, cooler than the rest of the house and grounded by its underground structure, provided the perfect setting. I put in my AirPods, switched to noise-canceling mode, queued up a brown noise playlist, closed my eyes—and let myself dissolve into emptiness.

October Check-In

Make four fall recipes √
Visit Ya Ya Farms √
Sign up for a hot yoga trial ○
Practice longer mediations √

In October, my focus on strengthening relationships in prior months—friend dates, low stakes social events, and cycling clinics— had begun to pay dividends. Scott and I ate dinner with the couple who hosted the September surprise party, enjoying an evening of laughter and incredibly fresh sushi. On another cool autumn Saturday morning, I met a longtime friend at a new café, where we indulged in pastries, something neither of us often allowed ourselves. I walked with a book club friend and with a cycling friend whose sweet dogs greeted me with wagging tails. Seven years after moving to the greater Denver area, I found myself thinking, *Whoa. I have people here!* My efforts to strengthen and expand relationships were…working.

And my connections were not just growing locally. I texted my cousin in Nashville to coordinate a spring visit with her. I called my sister in Oregon and told her I wanted to spend time with her and her family. When I arrived, the welcome basket from my nieces included delicious snacks, miniature toiletries, and a life-changing lavender lip balm. Together, we walked their dogs around the neighborhood and played Clue at the dining room table before dinner. The next morning, I sat on a kitchen stool drinking tea and listened to my nieces tell stories about friends, school, and dog shenanigans as they prepared their lunches. My sister and I drove to Cannon Beach and spent a long weekend enjoying local wine bars and restaurants, walking along the beach, and having deep, healing conversations over homemade soup and bread.

One early morning when I ran along the beach alone, I passed iconic Haystack Rock and thought I spotted…pirates. There was no pirate ship; the beach was empty except for me and…two pirates. They wore tricorne hats with feathers, hoop earrings, rings on every finger, long coats with buttons down the length of the front, and wide buttoned back cuffs. A sword was slung low at each of their hips, and one wore a musket. I walked up to them, and in my best Scottish brogue (don't know why I chose Scottish) said, "Permit me to take a picture of ye?"

The pirate said, "Argh. It shall cost you a gold coin." I took that as a "Yes," since I was not carrying gold bullion, took a picture, thanked them, and wished them well.

Tell you what—longer meditations.

Fifteen

November

- **Complete food log daily**
- **Practice flip turn**
- **Host Friendsgiving dinner**

I found myself drifting away from categorizing my activities. Did I still need that structure? Following the rhythms of the seasons began to feel more natural and less like cramming activities into arbitrary deadlines that nobody cared about but me. November was already shaping up to be a whirlwind. With projects to finish before visiting friends and family in December, our focus shifted to logistics—a new sliding door installation in the living room, shipping Christmas gifts, and packing for the month-long stay at an Airbnb in Palm Desert, California.

The *New Yorker* cartoon "Year-at-a-Glance" by Roz Chast captured the feeling perfectly: A pie graph represents the year, where each month represents a slice, albeit unequally. January is one third of the entire pie, March and February together form another third, and the remaining months May through December—where November and December are nearly invisible—comprise the last third.

Within two months, I would have been retired for an entire year. How had time moved so fast? Amidst the rush, I reminded myself that life was still made up of the small, ordinary moments—a simplicity that anchored my days and gave them shape.

Flogging and Flip Turns

During the summer, I had become complacent about food logging (flogging?) because I was so active—swimming, hiking, cycling, and walking with friends and dogs. But due to my elbow injury in October, my exercise routine shifted, and I wanted to be more mindful of balancing my intake with lower activity levels.

Body image and disordered eating are something I have struggled with. (Disordered?! My eating is quite orderly, thank you very much!) Fifteen years ago, I lost twenty pounds by logging food daily, a weight I have maintained. While food logging might seem tedious to some, it offers me a balance between freedom and control. Tracking my meals throughout the day keeps me aware of my calories and nutrition, helping me make intentional choices rather than second-guessing myself. It also allows me to monitor trends over time, noticing how certain foods affect my energy levels, sleep patterns, and digestion.

"Cronometer" is my favorite food logging app because of its extensive food library and custom meal and recipe feature. As part of Promoting Health and Wellness, I added food logging to my list—I wanted to return to the habit daily in November and start the holidays feeling healthy.

Because I eat oatmeal with chia seeds and fruit every day, I created custom meals for each variation—apple cinnamon almond butter, blackberry almond butter, and banana coconut cacao. This simple system not only lets me log breakfast with a single click but also ensures I stick to my committed fifteen grams of almond butter, preventing me from mindlessly adding extra.

Each bowl has its own small delight—the warmth of cinnamon and apples, sweet bananas against the deep richness of cacao, the tart of blackberries paired with creamy almond butter reminiscent of childhood PB&J. Even with routine, there is variety, something comforting yet flexible, much like the process of tracking itself.

Due to my elbow injury, I stopped cycling in October and swapped swimming for an ergonomic kickboard that didn't strain my neck while completing laps in the pool. Once my elbow healed, I planned to master a smooth underwater flip turn instead of my usual open turn—something I had watched fellow swimmers do. I had learned flip turns as a child but never swam on a team, so the skill faded over time.

As a member of Generation X, I have little patience for videos—I would rather read instructions and be done with it. The memes about reading cereal boxes at breakfast because we didn't have smartphones—100 percent accurate! To learn a flip turn, however, I made an exception. I watched YouTube videos that broke the technique into stages—getting comfortable with the flip, keeping my arms tight against my body, and positioning myself correctly on the wall. Following the first recommendation, I practiced doing flips mid-lane while keeping my arms close. I took in a bit of water through my nose and struggled to propel myself without using my hands—awkward but part of the process. My next step—doing the same flip while holding a kickboard in each hand to reinforce proper positioning—I planned to tackle during my next swim.

The universe chuckled.

On the last day of October, during my annual dermatology appointment, they biopsied two moles, and a week later, the office called. The mole on my thigh was stage-zero melanoma, and the mole on my back was precancerous. Both needed to be removed by excision within the month.

My surgeon explained the procedure: The surgeon would remove the visible mole plus 5 mm of surrounding healthy tissue to ensure the elimination of all cancer cells. Because of the skin's natural tension, they would also excise an area around the mole in the shape of a football to allow for proper wound closure with minimal puckering.

As I watched the surgeon draw the excision points on my thigh with a purple felt tip marker and manipulate my skin to visualize the closure, the gravity of the procedure hit me. My hands began to sweat, and I took deep breaths to remain calm. Afterward, as I gingerly climbed into the passenger seat, I admitted to Scott how drastically I had underestimated both the surgery and the recovery ahead.

At home, I followed the aftercare instructions—applying ice, alternating Tylenol and Advil—but even without prescription painkillers, I felt drugged. I had assumed that because the procedure only required local anesthesia, it was not a big deal. I was wrong. That first night, the pain—especially from the excision on my back—prevented me from moving enough to get comfortable and kept me awake. In bed, I sobbed quietly from the pain.

The second night, I managed a sponge bath with the giant disposable towelettes we use while camping, just as effective but much less fun than at the campsite. For three days, I barely left the sofa and watched *The Great British Baking Show* on Netflix. Our *Hamilton* tickets two days after the procedure went unused—I was too immobile and uncomfortable to go.

By the third night, removing the bandages and taking a shower felt life-affirming, and I slept well. By day four, I no longer needed Advil, though I limped around the house, careful not to stretch the incision site on my leg. Thankfully, the burning sensation in my back had faded.

Since our families live mostly in California and Scott and I do not travel around Thanksgiving, we decided to host a Friendsgiving dinner on Saturday before the holiday. Our friends usually traveled on the holiday to visit their families while we watched their dog, Remi. I initially felt excited about cooking—I printed recipes, made grocery lists, and created a countdown (yes, a spreadsheet) that began two days before the meal. But when I returned home from surgery, I quickly realized I would not be able to cook and would need to revise my plans. I texted our friends to let them know we would probably go to a restaurant instead.

To my surprise, the next day Scott announced he wanted to take over the cooking. I handed him six recipes—bone-in turkey breast with roasted vegetables, sausage cranberry stuffing, umami make-ahead gravy, cranberry apple chutney, pecan pie (brown sugar, not corn syrup!), and a buttery crust (no shortening!)—along with the grocery list and countdown schedule.

Scott dove into the countdown on Thursday, grocery shopping and making the cranberry chutney. On Friday, he made the gravy, baked the stuffing, and made a valiant, if somewhat comical, attempt at the pie crust. (Pro tip: Pie dough should not get hot in a food processor.) I limped into the kitchen to make a second crust.

Friendsgiving and the food turned out wonderfully! I felt better. Our friends brought a delicious fall salad and homemade whipped cream for the pecan pie, delectable with my "pinch hitter" crust. I felt over-whelmed with gratitude for my husband's care and support and for the kindness of our friends who always showed up with generosity. The event reminded me of the importance of leaning on the people we love and the deep comfort found in friendship, especially when life throws unexpected challenges our way. Friendsgiving or Thanksgiving, with its bounty, also reminded me that the dinner was not about a six-recipe countdown but about appreciating the privileges of being together, showing up, and sharing what we have.

Five days after my surgery, I began slowly walking our neighbor-hood trails. Gradually, my mobility returned as my sutures healed. I took longer walks and returned to easier Mirror barre classes in the basement.

It was not lost on me that, after the fear and anxiety associated with clipping in and falling on my bike, injury came from within my own body in the form of melanoma, likely fed by the vanity and carelessness of my teens and twenties. It was sobering. November was a month of recovery, reflection, and preparation—mending my body, quieting my mind, and tying up loose ends before the rush of the holidays swept in.

November Check-In

Complete food log daily ✓
Practice flip turn ◯
Host Friendsgiving dinner ✓

Sixteen

December

- **Sign up for hot yoga**
- **Bake three varieties of cookies**
- **Try a lucid dreaming app**
- **Create pit bull button**
- **Fika**

The first week of December, nearly two weeks after my surgeries, I felt healthy enough to take Remi for a morning walk in the snow. After our walk, while changing out of my exercise clothing, I noticed a rash under my arm. I assumed it was a heat rash, a reaction to wearing too many layers, and I spent the afternoon Christmas shopping in Old Town. By the evening, the rash had worsened, blistering and slightly painful. In the shower, I felt swollen, tender lymph nodes in my armpit.

The next morning, I called my healthcare provider, who was able to see me that day. I felt grateful because I often hear about friends and family members who must go to urgent care when their healthcare providers are scheduling a month out or longer. When I showed her the rash, she said, "Oh! That's shingles!"

I did not endure much pain in my skin, aside from a couple of blisters occasionally rubbing against my shirt, nor my nerves, often associated with the virus. Shingles lies dormant in our vertebrae after contracting chicken pox, typically triggered by stress or a weakened immune system, and most often affects adults over fifty. I had never chosen to get the shingles vaccine, thinking, "If I'm healthy and not stressed, why would I need that?"

The shingles diagnosis not only inconvenienced me, but my self-image also took a blow. I did not have a compromised immune system, and while nobody would describe me as easy-going, I did not typically feel anxious or stressed. Plus, I did all the things! Eight hours of sleep nightly, meditating and exercising daily, maintaining healthy body weight, blood pressure, and cholesterol, limiting caffeine and alcohol, and eating a plant-based diet. And I was retired! So, why now?

Shingles humbled me—a virus tied to advanced age and weakened immunity, neither of which aligned with my identity. I found myself reflecting on the past year, wondering if my body had been whispering warnings I had ignored or misread—recurring jaw pain, Temporomandibular Disorder (TMD) that mysteriously eased during the excisions, a persistent eyelid twitch in the fall quelled by reducing caffeine, nagging epicondylitis I dismissed as overuse, and knee pain I attributed to running. But then, I realized the flaws in my thinking. What? Was I going to look back and pathologize every eyelid twitch, jaw tick, and ache? I was healthy, but I was also middle-aged. I could not control everything with diet, exercise, sleep, and meditation. Whether based upon genetics, behavior, environment, or a complete unknown, sometimes…sh*t happens. And would continue to happen.

Just as we had the year before, Scott and I planned to spend December in Palm Desert. This time, we rented a small U-Haul trailer and spent two days filling it with bikes, hiking gear, and Christmas presents. Normally, the desert drive is beautiful, but with shingles, it was misery—the seatbelt rubbed against blisters, the sun seared through the windshield despite layers of clothing, and even cranking the A/C higher didn't help.

But I had packed salvation for lunch—the most delicious sand-wiches in the world. On slices of homemade craisin pecan bread, I piled turkey, stuffing, gravy, and cranberry chutney left over from Friends-giving. We groaned in delight as we ate. I imagine, for dinner, normal people stop at the nearest restaurant on a road trip. Not me—I made a curry. At a Courtyard Marriott in Utah, after we parked the trailer and settled in, we chilled a bottle of Sauvignon Blanc and walked across the street to pick up naan and rice from the Indian restaurant I had ordered en route. Back in the room, we heated the curry, squeezed lemon over it, and savored it with crisp wine and warm bread. Delicious.

***

I had been pushing yoga aside for eleven months due to travel, price and proximity, stress injuries, and then shingles. In December, in Palm Desert, I finally signed up for a month of Bikram yoga—my first yoga classes in three years. I mentioned to the instructor that the first class might be difficult for me, and he replied, "Starting the day with some-thing difficult makes everything after seem easy."

The 104-degree heat hit me like a wall as I entered the room. I had initially forgotten about breath of fire, the breath control technique typ-ically performed at the start of Bikram yoga classes. I felt strong as I transitioned into poses, aligning myself as instructed throughout the ninety-minute class. While I could not recall some of the asanas, my body remembered them, so I trusted it. And I kept returning.

Though not the most physically demanding, asana number twenty-two—camel pose—made me feel the worst. Camel pose is a deep back-bend that opens the chest, lifts the heart, and arches the back, and despite its physical challenges, I also experience its benefits. By the time we reach this pose, the room sizzles at maximum heat. I sometimes become lightheaded, my body's way of signaling when I have inadequately hy-drated the day prior or eaten too late in the morning. Camel pose—lean-ing back, opening the heart, and letting go of control—is a literal surrender. The terrible feeling shifts to extraordinary in a moment, all traces of anger leaving my body as I stare up at the smoke alarm.

Once the sequence of asanas was completed and we lay in savasana—corpse pose—a tranquil feeling washed over me, and I savored the stillness, allowing my body to go limp in the heat.

The tranquil feeling did not result solely from sweaty asanas in 104-degree heat. I had crossed to the other side of something. I was healing—the shingles rash from earlier in the month had disappeared, and though the skin surrounding the incisions felt numb, the scars thinned and lightened day by day. They would fade, just as my need to manage outcomes and control every detail was beginning to fade—I could schedule classes on calendars, weigh grams of food on digital scales, and monitor virtually everything from my Apple Watch. Or not.

Virtual Fikas, Lucid Dreams, Crinkled Cookies, and W-Shaped Grins

Though I had completed only a few activities around Strengthening and Expanding Relationships, the activities I did complete taught me that I could create friendships from acquaintances with whom I shared a common interest—neighbors and club members—or revive, maintain, and strengthen them. For December, I opted to focus on the latter.

Fika (fee-ka'), an everyday tradition in Swedish life, is a chance to connect with others over coffee, often accompanied by pastries—or, in my case, Christmas cookies. And really, shouldn't more activities in life be accompanied by pastry? Fika can happen during the workday with a quick ten-minute break, or during time with friends and stretch out for much longer.

The idea of a virtual Fika came from a Substack post by *Creative Fuel* writer Anna Brones, who also wrote a book about Fika. The word comes from the Swedish word kaffi (coffee), banned multiple times throughout Swedish history, so people invented a secret word to gather for coffee—hence, "fika."

I have friends spread across different states whom I don't see in person regularly, but I wanted to strengthen those connections beyond text messages. I reached out to a friend to see if she wanted to meet for a virtual coffee chat over FaceTime or Zoom in December or after the holiday chaos. My suggestion was a thirty-minute chat—enough time to catch up but not so much that it would require complicated scheduling. If the conversation ran longer, that was okay too.

I set up my first virtual fika for the second week of December, connecting with my longtime friend and former roommate on FaceTime, and we talked for over an hour. We caught up on everything from our parents' recent health challenges to her daughter's pursuits in Texas, including the intense world of gymnastics. I shared updates on my recent injuries, surgeries, and health struggles, and we discussed the usual holiday stresses—travel, family, and everything in between.

This virtual fika not only allowed me to maintain a meaningful connection but also reinforced the importance of nurturing and reviving long-distance friendships—proving that even a simple chat can deepen bonds and keep relationships thriving, no matter the distance. I promptly texted a friend in Pennsylvania to arrange a January fika.

* * *

Though I wore my Apple Watch while sleeping, I did not pay much attention to the sleep tracker details. The Apple Watch sleep tracker offers several features: You can set a sleep goal, activate Sleep Focus to minimize distractions, and set a bedtime reminder. It also tracks your sleep history, breaking it into stages and comparing it to previous nights. Using motion sensors, heart rate monitors, and other biometrics—like blood oxygen levels, respiratory rate, noise detection, and skin temperature changes—the watch provides a detailed picture of sleep patterns.

Dreaming apps monitor these vitals to determine dreaming states. We cycle through REM and non-REM stages, and dreams typically occur during REM sleep. When it detects a dreaming state, typically reached in REM stages, the app alerts the dreamer with a tactile or audible signal. This interruption can either make the dreamer aware they are dreaming or wake the dreamer to return to the dream, both of which tend to induce lucid dream states.

I typically remember at least one dream each night, but I felt curious to recall more, as my intuition spoke to me through my dreams. When I did remember them, my dreams presented in Technicolor, Dolby sound, Aromavision…all the senses plus a couple extra. Sometimes my dreams were lucid. In my dreams, I regularly visited burrito stands, appetizer cafés, and sushi bars that did not, as far as I knew, exist in waking life. At least I hope not, because one sushi bar served human sashimi. Anyway…I saw recurring characters—dead people who ate charcuterie and shared their regrets, celebrities in their kitchen who wanted "regular friends," politicians who…(let's just leave that out), and of course, talking dogs.

I downloaded the app but immediately became concerned with privacy implications after viewing its agreements. In addition to the health data sensitivity, I did not know where the data was stored. Its need for access to the microphone to capture vocalizations was a step too far. I wondered if poorly configured permissions could allow other apps access to sleep data without explicit consent. All that access, especially nightly and in my bed, felt intrusive. Not at all restful. I was not in the mood to think through the various privacy implications and promptly deleted the app.

***

To wrap up the year, I wanted to focus more on Fostering Joy and Creativity as I had completed so few creative projects. Well, unless I included writing a book that provided an account of neglected creative projects!

I love baking cookies, but I love eating them even more! Definitely a part of the Fostering Joy and Creativity category but most certainly not Promoting Health and Wellness. For the past few Christmases, I have baked three different recipes: Chai Snickerdoodles, Maple Frosted Brown Sugar Cookies, and a guest cookie. The guest cookies were unremarkable. The World's Best Cookie was a dull shortbread that definitely did not live up to its name. The Magic Bar was less than magic, despite its decadent ingredients. And the Biscoff Cookie Butter Cookie barely hinted of cookie butter flavor, leaving them far from memorable.

This year, I wanted to find a cookie worthy of joining the ranks of my favorites. I had a few contenders in mind: a ginger molasses sandwich cookie, Milk Bar's famous Compost Cookie, and a bright, sunny *New York Times* Lemon Turmeric Crinkle Cookie. With my parents visiting, I decided to bake the Lemon Turmeric Crinkle Cookie, knowing my mom is a huge lemon fan. The turmeric was a natural ingredient to impart a vibrant yellow hue, with no discernible flavor. Fresh out of the oven, the cookies tasted good—but, like every guest cookie before them, they were unremarkable.

Maybe there was no perfect third cookie. Maybe unremarkable guest cookies simply allowed me to appreciate Chai Snickerdoodles and Maple Frosted Brown Sugar Cookies. Perhaps finding joy in baking is not always about perfection but about nostalgia and the act of baking, trying new recipes, and the satisfaction of sharing something made with care.

***

The pit bull button badge I had originally planned to create in March, I had rescheduled for December. I thought it would be a fun, creative project with the potential to help pit bulls find fur-ever homes. My concept was like a Trap, Neuter, Vaccinate, Release (TNVR) button I had created while volunteering for an organization focused on feral cats. The distinctive tipped ear signals to future rescuers that the cat has been neutered.

I wanted to use simple shapes and lines to convey the distinctive smile of pit bulls. Their most recognizable feature were their W-shaped grins that perfectly captured the joyful essence of these dogs. I spent a few mornings experimenting with Apple Pages shape functions, but I couldn't quite capture the lovable expressions using simple vector shapes—it seemed that the lines of their faces were better captured by freeform doodles, and I likely required different software for that. I did not finish the button in December, but I decided to keep trying—sometimes the most joyful things are the hardest to capture and require patience.

December Check-In

Join Bikram yoga √
Bake ~~three varieties of~~ cookies √
Try a lucid dreaming app ○
Create pit bull button ○
Fika √

Q4 Retrospective

I had begun Q4 with a renewed vigor as the weather cooled and my summer activities eased. Small acts of soul attention—longer meditations, food logging, a bike fitting—did not yield immediate results, but they supported my well-being. Though melanoma and shingles created painful and unwelcome interruptions, they became what I allowed them to be. I scheduled my shingles vaccinations and quarterly skin checks with gratitude for my healthcare, my providers, and loved ones that helped me heal.

I was finding a sense of balance—among my activities, my values, my commitments, and how I felt. Learning to play piano, clipping in, or planting a garden—no single pursuit defined me. That realization brought a sense of ease, though I recognized that too much time without a meaningful focus could leave me feeling untethered. And while too many pursuits sometimes led to burnout, I had found a steady rhythm, not quite a rush—possibly even flow.

And I was writing. I told Uber drivers and the occasional fellow cyclists that I was working on a book, but few people in my inner circle knew. Most will hear about it only after the fact, in a text with a link to the finished project. They will be surprised. They will say, "I didn't even know you were writing!" This is by design. I have always carried what I call dark horse energy.

Maybe it didn't feel safe to want something so much—to finish and then publish a book—because not achieving it would hurt. Like in eighth grade, when I lost the ASB President election, or as a senior, when college rejection letters arrived before the acceptances. They were not just my losses; others who believed in me witnessed the unexpected failure—friends who wore my campaign buttons, parents who took me to tour campuses, teachers who wrote glowing recommendations. That exposure stung more than the failure itself.

For years I had wanted it this way: To fumble around in the dark by myself, knowing that whatever I was working on may never see the light of day, only to toss a *ta-dah!* Molotov cocktail over my shoulder if I succeeded. To struggle in the harsh daylight—being messy, painting ugly acrylics, playing the wrong notes, tipping over while clipped in, failing—was to open myself up to…I wasn't sure what. It was more than criticism or judgment. Was it a failed heroine's journey? A vicarious deflation? It was difficult to name. So, I sat on our peacock blue sofa, drank tea, and pinned capsule wardrobes or tiny homes while writing in my dream journal, something private, safe, and unseen.

It was a type of cruel optimism, wanting to do a thing—a non-specific, creative endeavor of an extraordinary outcome—hoping to emerge with it, unscathed and without criticism, injury, or scars. This way of thinking not only deprived me of the joy of doing all the things but also deprived me of connection with others—their experience and wisdom, camaraderie, and companionship.

But slowly, wanting something—and admitting it while working toward it—stopped feeling dangerous. Over early morning texts and cups of tea, I told friends about the progress of what I finally called *my book*. On the trail, friends asked how it was going. On gravel roads, feet pedaling and legs pumping, I said, "I'm writing a book about retirement from a woman's point of view."

And each time, the people around me listened. They held space. They asked questions. They cared. They were rooting for me.

And that felt good.

Seventeen

Sucking at New Things

I have always appreciated a level of change and novelty—even disruption—in my life. It is difficult to imagine a life not rife with change—moving cities and changing careers. Being asked about my leisure activities at the Shangri-La Hotel in Singapore kickstarted a desire not to just change cities but to change myself. Life in Los Angeles felt constricted—not just by traffic, crowds, or a lack of nature but by how tightly I lived within my loop of work, workouts, and life logistics. I wanted to live a richer life when I returned stateside.

Disruptions bring change and uncertainty, something humans are generally hard-wired against. By the time we reach retirement, many of us have often spent years mastering a profession or settling into familiar routines. For some, stepping into unfamiliar territory can create a level of fear or shame if we struggle or feel incompetent. New people, places, and skill sets can create stress and feed our fears—unsettling as newness disrupts routines, shifts identity, and introduces a future that may feel uncharted.

According to Marc Lewis of *The Guardian*, humans find uncertainty so stressful that we prefer a known negative outcome over an unknown outcome. Rather than sit with uncertainty, our minds spin stories of failure or disaster—catastrophizing—as if predicting the worst will somehow make it easier to bear. Imagining my own disastrous injuries kept me from clipping in for many years.

And yet, despite a preference for certainty, the human brain remains flexible and adaptive. Daniel Graham, Ph.D., author of *An Internet in Your Head*, describes the routing system in our brains as resembling an internet, which makes us flexible. This flexibility persists well into old age and makes it normal to change our behaviors, thoughts, actions, and even habits at almost any stage of life—we are never truly stuck because our minds are wired for reinvention, regardless of age.

So, while we may dread change and grumble as it happens, we most likely will be able to handle it. And chances are that we will like the changes—maybe even a lot. In retirement, this flexibility can be our superpower—we can try painting, or pottery, or learn to make pasta just because we feel like it. Research says our brains will simply move synapses around to create space.

I chose to leave behind the feelings of constraint in California. When I moved to Colorado nearly eight years ago, I had planned to take up new outdoor hobbies, volunteer, and join social organizations to find my tribe. I said, "Colorado is no longer just a place; it's a state of mind."

I learned to embrace the freedom to be a beginner, to try things, fail, and abandon what did not hit the mark. I began entirely without guilt, regret, or even shame. I told myself, *Be brave enough to suck at something new.* In doing so, I realized that the singular focus and natural gifts I once envied in others began to look—at least in retirement—less like something to aspire to and more like a type of prison. A tyranny of passion can lock people into identities, a beautifully admired golden cage. At a certain point, people do not just do the thing—they are the thing. I began to appreciate the benefits of my curiosity, dilettantism, and even obscurity.

And I kept choosing new things. Some things I sucked at, and some things…well, they just kind of sucked. I attended a knitting group and kept losing stitches—if a knitting circle was not compelling enough to keep me interested, knitting solo held even less interest. I attended a mountain bike clinic that—though beginner—still felt too technical. I volunteered with hospice and found it unpredictable. I volunteered virtually writing grants for a non-profit but found I preferred walking dogs in-person to writing about cats virtually. I tried to make friends using an app and found it awkward. I tried adult coloring books, and they bored me. Besides, coloring inside the lines was something I could be *less* good at.

But I also sucked at new things that turned out okay. I returned to skiing after thirty years, fell, cried because I was scared, and took lessons until skiing became both serene and thrilling, especially during weekdays on nearly abandoned groomed runs. I tried gravel biking and liked it, away from cars, enjoying the scenery of country roads and the wildlife that scurried across my path and flew overhead. I ran two charity 5K races and continued running on trails near my home, where I found packed snow an ideally cool and spongy surface. I was abysmal at growing radishes but successful enough with cherry tomatoes. I tried vinyasa yoga but fell in love with Bikram.

With each new activity, I learned that the flip side of sucking at something new was a lack of attachment to being the best—or even good—at anything. And, oh—did this offer freedom! My identity was not tied to achieving success, so I let myself begin badly at nearly everything I attempted. As such, barriers to entry lowered for me. I felt perfectly comfortable sucking at every new thing! And that didn't suck at all.

This made me more flexible and less attached to habits. When a closed pool thwarted my morning plans to swim, I returned home to cycle. If it was too windy to cycle, I ran the trail along the creek. And if it was too warm to run, I headed to our cool basement for a Mirror Barre workout. When my elbow injury necessitated, I did not swim or cycle for a month, but I used a kickboard in the pool and a stationary bike at the rec center. Instead of feeling frustrated—or rather, instead of allowing frustration to ruin my workout—I did something different. I learned to pivot.

While meditating one evening, I had an epiphany about how I had changed during my first year of retirement. Whenever I imagined trying a new activity or learning a new skill, I pictured my current self, transported into the future—already riding clipped in on single-track trails or playing Beethoven on my weighted keyboard. The image intimidated me. And because of that, I often procrastinated—I hesitated to buy the clips or to schedule the lessons. But my vision was flawed. It assumed I would leap from inexperience to expertise without becoming all the versions of myself in between.

As Alice in Wonderland says, "I can't go back to yesterday, because I was a different person then." She's not wrong. When I imagined my future self, I forgot about the many days in between—days where I simply put on a hoodie, walked down to our chilly basement, and practiced scales and simple songs for thirty or forty-five minutes. Over time, those songs became more complex. And so did I.

In some ways, it reminded me of software projects. When we released a product, we didn't jump straight from version 1.0 to 2.0. We rolled out 1.0.1, 1.0.2, then maybe 1.1, 1.1.1…you get the idea. There are incremental updates, not overnight transformations. The point is that there are always versions and iterations—slow progress happening behind the scenes. Practicing scales in the basement did not look glamorous, but it was version 1.0.1 of learning to play Beethoven. Clumsy, persistent, necessary.

And this rule of iterations wasn't just true for training, practicing, or even software. It applied to everything. Every day, I read books and blog posts, listened to podcasts, watched animals, picked hornworms off tomato plants, painted and drew badly, talked with people—paid attention.

And each time, I brought a new version of myself: a little braver and a little less attached to getting it right. I let go of anything performative and instead dwelled in the present. Like Alice, I was "curiouser and curiouser," stepping further away from productivity and perfectionism and deeper into…just being.

I created my List of Likes to begin tracking what I might enjoy in retirement. I created categories to align my retirement "likes" with my core values—research said I would be more likely to continue donating blood if I believed I was Making the World a Better Place, not just completing a task. When guided by values, choices and behaviors link to psychological well-being according to *Psychology Today* writer Jessica Koehler, Ph.D. They reduce internal conflicts and lead to a more meaningful and authentic life.

So…had I accomplished that? Had I created a more meaningful and authentic life, found my ikigai or dharma, or at the very least pursued enjoyable activities in an intentional way? Well, for sure I had learned a few lessons in the past year.

Promoting Health and Wellness

Health and wellness, I learned, was nothing short of witchcraft. No matter how much care I took today to eat well, exercise, sleep, and practice mindfulness, sometimes, the call was coming from inside the house. Despite my best efforts, illness originated from within, and I could not travel through time to apply higher SPF to my younger self. My physician found another melanoma during my February three-month checkup, and that diagnosis once again relegated me to the sofa for two days of *The Great British Baking Show*. Though the second excision hurt less, the fear remained, but at least, the second time around, I had a shingles vaccine.

I continued to schedule skin checks every three months, and while I hoped my provider would discover no additional melanomas, it reminded me that every day was precious. It also made me more proactive about my healthcare. I knew that, despite my healthy lifestyle, I was immune to nothing, and this made me more vigilant and more willing to ask for additional tests when something felt not quite right. I would not grow complacent, assuming that symptoms resulted from aging. Too many people I had known were sent away from doctors' offices with simmering symptoms that turned into death sentences. And I also knew that being able to advocate for myself—and be heard—was its own kind of privilege, one not afforded to everyone.

Other health and wellness lessons carried less gravitas. Most activities—cold plunges, food logging, meditation—simply required prioritization and a bit of habit stacking, like logging meals after lunch or meditating immediately following a post-workout stretch. More ambitious pursuits—restarting Bikram yoga and swimming or training for blue gravel rides—demanded daily planning and coordinating use of our shared car. These were not just habits to fit in; they were commitments that shaped my days.

Making the World a Better Place

Was I doing enough? Was I doing things that mattered? The thoughts made me sad—then angry—then sad again. Since 1970, the planet has seen a catastrophic 73 percent decline in wildlife. The primary driver? Our global food system—livestock to feed humans and grain to feed livestock—which fuels habitat loss, degradation, and over-harvesting. These in turn accelerate invasive species, climate change, and disease.

I wish I could say I found peace reflecting on my small acts of conservation or that I turned to a cache of inspirational quotes for reassurance, but I did not. I could only sit in the discomfort of my knowing, while at the same time refusing to let it paralyze me. I would plant a pollinator garden the following year and continue volunteering, walking dogs, and filling medical supplies. And I would continue to ask myself if I was doing enough and doing things that mattered.

In the post "Less Think, More Do" from her Substack *Peak Notions*, author Laura Kennedy writes a haunting passage that captures what she calls "the uncomfortable dissonance of doing what little good you can." It gutted me.

> Sometimes the disincentive against doing what you can is how deeply uncomfortable and inadequate it feels. The way that it forces you to confront the reality that you could always do more, or better. If you don't wade into that morass, resigning suffering to some theoretical realm, pushing it as far from you as possible, then you don't have to meet that reality. You don't have to confront the ways you fail to look it in the eye. You don't have to figure out what to do with the painful ideas and feelings that generates, dangling from you like useless limbs.

Expanding and Strengthening Relationships

Every book and article I read about retirement addressed the importance of social connections—as our careers and accomplishments fade into the background, our relationships become our most important asset.

Arthur C. Brooks, author of *From Strength to Strength*, references the Harvard Study of Adult Development that began in 1938 and continues today, tracking health and happiness across generations—for men. Seven predictors contributed to place participants in the happy/well category versus the sad/sick category: smoking, alcohol abuse, obesity, sedentary lifestyle, coping styles, education, and relationships.

The surprise finding of the study was how much close relationships affected participants. The single most important trait among happy/well elders is healthy relationships. Relationships that best mitigate loneliness are typically a primary romantic relationship and friendships—

people satisfied with their relationships at age fifty were the healthiest at age eighty. Equally important, Brooks points out, is that our spouses cannot be our only relationship, comparing it to a poorly diversified investment portfolio. A single primary relationship is a recipe for loneliness—death or divorce can leave a person single and without friends.

Simply put, "Loneliness kills. It's as powerful as smoking or alcoholism," says the director of the study, Psychiatrist Robert Waldinger.

While, more than anything, I hoped that Scott and I would grow old together, it made me happy that we were building separate friendships. I had chosen Expanding and Strengthening Relationships as one of my core values with intentions to see more of my family, strengthen my existing friendships in California, and develop local friendships in Colorado.

Despite some initial snafus over the holidays coordinating visits with longtime friends, I felt happy with my efforts and results. We made time to visit friends and family, even if only to spend an afternoon catching up over lunch. In-person visits, if only once a year, made me feel closer to them. Throughout the year, not only did I make efforts to spend time with my parents, but an extended visit with my sister dissolved old tensions and created a stronger bond. Our communication became regular and spontaneous, richer and more in-depth. I knew that, when I called, she would pick up if only to say, "Give me ten minutes, and I'll call you back." And she did.

I struggled more than I expected to build new relationships—not because it was difficult, but because I was in the habit of doing things alone, squeezing activities into whatever gaps my schedule allowed. As usual, I was overthinking it—imagining I needed to join a yoga class or sign up for pickleball to meet people. Proximity goes a long way in forming friendships. When I finally texted neighbors or book club members to get together, the ease of connection it brought surprised me.

I reminded myself to stay flexible and leave space. If I had planned to swim in the morning but was invited to walk, I said yes to the walk and shifted my swim to the afternoon. When a friend suggested a field trip to see an exhibit, I said yes to that too. I attended Bonsai Bar and learned the essentials of bonsai care, styling, and maintenance—on a school night.

Though the book club I started a year before retirement gained and lost members, the core group of founding women remained. Month after month, we gathered, drinking wine, sharing charcuterie, rarely talking about the books. We listened to each other's hard days and offered comfort. We picked up mail, let dogs out, and kept watch when someone was away—not just proverbial cat-feeders, but true friends, women I am grateful to know and spend time with.

Early morning conversations, albeit over text, were a continuous reminder that long-standing friendships weathered time, distance, and change. Sometimes I scheduled fikas with out-of-state friends I had not seen in a while, and while it was sometimes tricky to pin people down for days and times to talk, I eventually did, and my patience was rewarded with the opportunity to spend an hour together, uninterrupted by daily life.

Scott asked me how I compared my capacity for friendships now to my capacity for friendships while working.

"Was it like starting to diversify your portfolio years prior to retirement," he asked, "or was it more like diving into it once you retired because you had more capacity?"

Though, clearly, I had more time to meet with friends now, I had not considered the similarities between diversifying my portfolio and building a network of friends prior to retirement. But Scott was right: My quarterly culture dates with a colleague began post-Covid as annual lunches and Christmas shopping. My first ride with my cycling group took place in May 2021. I began volunteering in 2022, and in 2023, I started the book club. Not all of these efforts culminated in friendships, but many did.

The feelings that come with social bonds—whether deepening existing friendships or sharing spontaneous conversations with loose ties—are deeply satisfying, but where and how those bonds form can be unpredictable. When it came to Expanding and Strengthening Relationships, maintaining friendships was easiest, reviving old ones was surprisingly natural, and turning acquaintances with shared interests into friends felt organic. Yet, simply attending an event or joining an organization did not guarantee connection. I learned that friendship could not be forced—it had to unfold.

I had wondered if retirement itself was sexist—if all the books about identity loss and restlessness were written for men. A year in, I still couldn't say. But stepping away from the culture of meetings, deliverables, and budget projections, I began to notice something else: Without seeking it, I had gathered a circle of wise women—instructors and coaches, practitioners and therapists, artists and athletes. They held space for me, and their wisdom slowly became my own.

Find your tribe. Celebrate your wins. Pay attention to melody. Notice the gifts. Find stillness. Loosen your grip to absorb the shock. Turn your head where you want to go. The wheels want to turn—let them.

Letting go of my old frameworks, I had found something new—wait for it—a damework.

Fostering Joy and Creativity

I assumed that once I was retired and had time for activities that brought me joy, I would just…you know…do them. But I did not always do that. As it turns out, committing to activities solely for the sake of joy is time-consuming and requires significant mental energy. For eleven months, I struggled to add Bikram yoga—one of my most favorite activities ever—into my life. I never took a painting class, designed a dress, or attended a Sur La Table cooking class. Anything that fell into my creative category, I typically pushed aside first.

I noticed that joy didn't require more, but less—less pressure, fewer expectations, more permission to simply be. I found unexpected joy in taking things less seriously and committing to less—not more—and the month of June served as an example of this. I bought fresh flowers, wore summer dresses while running errands, and incorporated seasonal farket summer fruits and vegetables into our meals. These were not activities I initially identified as likes, but they added a layer of lightness and texture to my days, as I appreciated the cyclical and ephemeral nature of the seasons. In choosing small pleasures over grand plans, I rediscovered something I had not expected: Joy, when quiet, feels deeper.

I had once imagined fostering creativity solely through structured pursuits like painting classes and piano lessons, but finding a Jungian therapist laid a deeper foundation. Dreamwork reminded me that life is cyclical, continuously shifting, and that clinging too tightly to a fixed way of being was both futile and unhealthy. Understanding my dreams—and, in turn, my subconscious—helped me react less, notice more, and stay curious in the face of change.

Fostering Joy and Creativity, I learned, could be both effortless and elusive. The simplest moments brought me joy—on a walk in my neighborhood, two bald eagles soared overhead, low and close enough that I felt the air shift beneath their massive wings. I watched them glide across the creek and back again, honored to witness their courtship. Had I fostered that moment? Perhaps. I was in nature where I felt most alive, and I had intentionally left my AirPods at home. Sometimes fostering joy was as simple as making space for it.

Yet, in my efforts to Foster Joy and Creativity, I could not ignore my lack of spontaneity. Noticing this caused me to ponder the irony of trying to plan for spontaneity—an almost paradoxical endeavor that highlighted just how much I struggled to loosen my grip on structure. In the future, I hoped to let go of the need for complete control, embracing the unpredictability that could allow for unexpected moments of joy and creativity. Maybe I could set an intention to be spontaneous and track my spontaneous moments in a spreadsheet!

And what about the activities I did not complete and crossed off my list? I learned lessons there too. When I was already engaged in similar activities that met the same needs, I tended to forgo new ones. For example, I never tried pickleball because I swam and cycled, and adding another physical activity felt unnecessary. It made more sense to deepen what I was already doing.

Some activities, like learning a flip turn or eating dinner outside, simply became impractical. Summer winds kept us from dining under the umbrella in June, and surgery in November sidelined most of my efforts late in the year. But I knew those would resurface when the timing improved.

Then, there were activities I abandoned completely—a lucid dreaming app and pairing my Garmin with my Apple Watch. Both were part of my Et Pourquoi Pas category—ideas driven more by curiosity than alignment with my core values. Not wrong, just extra.

Eighteen

Drawer Space for Joy

Maybe, at the start of the year, I needed to prove I would not fall into retirement tropes. I initially shaped my experiment with lists, spreadsheets, and calendars, familiar artifacts I had relied upon while working as a project manager to plan predictable outcomes. I created them for my year-long experiment as I had learned to do throughout my career. I had subconsciously created a framework of intentions for others to approve, and then I presented completed deliverables—proof of success. It served as scaffolding, providing a safe, stable platform that allowed me to try new things, fail, write about them, and then try other new things. I lined up all the things I would do—gathered from my List of Likes—to complete and check off.

But I realized it was a kind of spiritual bypass, my own defense against boredom or identity loss, a security blanket of busyness and structure. That list—so tidy, so intentional—was still tied to outcomes and still rooted in the same work culture I claimed to be leaving behind, another project to manage and another attempt to prove my usefulness. They were artifacts in the truest sense of the word, structures not naturally present in the matter being observed but formed by artificial means. Each activity tucked neatly into a category and assigned to a month. But as the year progressed, I grew to trust my intuition and internal rhythms, and I slowly dismantled the scaffolding. It no longer fit.

In June, slipping into summer dresses and picking up tomatoes at the farmers market helped me savor the season. Later in the year, visiting Ya Ya Farms and reacquainting myself with butternut squash and pumpkin recipes stirred my excitement for fall. Slowing down and tuning into the rhythms of each season brought joy by pulling me into the present moment.

Creative projects, though often the first to slip when my schedule overflowed, brought levity when I made space for them—whether I made a batch of surprisingly good Lekker Bars or painted gloriously bad acrylics. Sometimes I found steady satisfaction in small improvements like cleaning out a cupboard, upgrading my swim goggles, or getting a proper bike fitting. These incremental upgrades—practical but purposeful—wove a sense of progress into my months.

The outcomes—whether finally joining Bikram, trying the cold plunge pool, or setting up a fika—even if they were initially dressed up in work clothes, had been in service to my soul. Unlike the tasks and projects I had completed in the past, these came from me and belonged to me. They were ideas I had been brewing under the surface for years leading up to retirement, not hobbies suggested by others who thought I might enjoy the strategy of chess or the peaceful tactility of knitting. My activities emerged from a deeper place, pointing toward the person I wanted to become—a person who donates blood, grows vegetables, finds her tribe, and makes summer salads with seasonal farket produce.

A rhythm began to unfold. Each month, I chose one activity that stretched me—something challenging, expansive, or brave. Then, I added a second, one that invited creativity or welcomed something new. I looked for a way to savor the season in front of me and another to make space for connection with someone else. And finally, I sought stillness. This rhythm—anchoring my days in challenge, creativity, connection, and rest—allowed me to reflect on other frameworks I had once turned to for guidance.

One was ikigai, a concept I had been chasing since I first began thinking seriously about retirement. At first, it inspired me—the idea of aligning what you love, what you are good at, what the world needs, and what you can be paid for. But over time, it began to feel oddly constraining, especially in this new phase of life. A core tenet of ikigai is usefulness—that what you do should serve some need in the world. But that idea, that the world must need it, started to feel like another weight to carry. Producing something needed by the world, that nebulous *out there*…I was tired of letting it shape me.

Years ago, a therapist asked me, "Why do you keep trying to be useful?" Her question still echoes—haunting me, helping me. Being still, slowing down, and resisting the urge to be useful—or more specifically, to be productive—has never come naturally to me. I had been in the habit of checking off tasks instead of being present. I even had to earn rest—justify it by prior effort. Napping was "doing something," timed at twenty minutes.

Though it is easy to fault our fast-paced culture, this compulsion toward productivity has roots in our experiences. When members of Gen X were kids, authority figures expected us to be useful—from household chores to part-time jobs—learning by doing, often without supervision or structured schedules. Participation trophies were unheard of, and rewards were earned. Our generation made do and stayed useful, fitting into the available spaces, a near pathological desire to contribute, as if to justify our very existence.

My sister and I still talk about after-school chores waiting for us— vacuuming, dishes, laundry. Typically, no one was home. It was the '80s. We watched *The Brady Bunch* reruns until we heard the Pinto in the driveway. Then—reflexively—we switched off the TV and disappeared into our bedrooms. A habitual bracing set in. Today, we laugh about it—even now, if we hear a car pull into the garage, we feel the impulse to jump up off the sofa, hide snacks, and mill about the kitchen sink, tidying.

Usefulness—often framed as practical, efficient, or resourceful—is seen as a virtue. It is praised. Once a situational strength, it eventually becomes the lens through which we measure our worth. It turns into a default mode of identity, an internalized performance. We struggle to simply be because our instinct is always to do. My narrative of time and space was shaped over half a lifetime not just by careers and their orbit but by a culture that continually expected all of us to do more.

A year ago, I jumped off the hedonic treadmill, stopped playing Tetris, and focused on the intrinsic. The shapes stopped falling. The gaping spaces often felt uncomfortable.

There was some irony to it, really, creating an outcome-based framework to feel useful, and then having it lead me to what I had been looking for: a level of purpose and space for my ideas to take form. Not just space in my schedule but in my mind, in my identity. I gave myself permission to want something just for the joy of it—and then to act on it.

Coincidentally, Scott emailed me designs for our closet. As I looked over the drawings, we talked about our current setup—how I used a dresser in the bedroom, and he used one in the closet.

"My socks occupy just a corner of the drawer with my workout clothes. It's okay but not ideal," I said.

"Since we're starting fresh, maybe we should approach this from the ideal," Scott said.

I had carte blanche—and at first, I was thrown. But then, I realized the closet design was a metaphor. Prior to retirement, I had been a woman who squeezed in trail runs or piano practice between conference calls or in the forty minutes before dinner. I had been a woman who read Marie Kondo's book and then rolled my socks tightly to fit into whatever space was available. I had folded myself into the in-between spaces—between meetings, between meals, between where I thought I was expected to be. My joy had been rolled tight like socks pressed into the corner of a drawer.

But now, I was learning to build space—not just find it. I was becoming a woman who said, "I need a sock drawer." I have hiking socks, cycling socks, running socks, barre socks (the kind with grip), dress socks…and F-word socks. They deserved their own space—a dedicated drawer. Just as I would add a drawer bank to our closet to allow my socks to take up space, I would allow my joy to take up space. And not just a drawer. My joy was no longer tidy; it was expansive and uncontained, spilling out of the closet, out of the house, and into the open space.

My joy was unbound.

THE END

Acknowledgments

I am grateful to my early readers, Walker Stafford and Emmily Hobbs, whose sharp questions and specific feedback kept parts of this book from wandering off into the weeds. And to Sandy Willens and Sena Cooper—thank you for your persistent "How's the book coming?" inquiries, which served as both encouragement and gentle surveillance.

A special nod to Debbie Hobbs, who, while standing in her driveway, told me I should write a book. I'm still not sure whether she meant it as inspiration or an exit strategy to get me to the airport, but either way, here we are.

To Dad, who coached my sister and me through skiing, bike-riding, tennis, fishing, and all things outdoors—even when I would have much preferred to stay inside and read—thank you for teaching patience, the value of sucking at something before you get better, and how to keep trying anyway, even through all the tears I shed along the way.

To Mom—chauffeur, pastry chef, costume designer, event planner, and art director—whose exacting eye and late-night proofreading sessions on my high-school papers involved raised voices, crying, and more red ink than I thought possible, thank you for helping me take writing seriously and for somehow encouraging the idea of a creative life.

Thank you to Lisa Glatt, my writing instructor from long ago, who spotted and praised my unique voice long before I knew what to do with it.

To Penelope Trunk, whose brutally honest critiques of my truly awful blog posts sometimes made me wince—she insisted I write about what hurts—thank you for pushing me past boredom into something real.

To the Boulder Writers Group where I learned about self-publishing (for ourselves, primarily, but still)—thank you for the camaraderie and reminder that writing is something we keep choosing, one Saturday at a time.

Thank you to my editor Brianna McCabe, whose confirmation that this was indeed a real book reduced me to happy tears. Thank you to my copyeditor, Andie Carver, and proofreader Brooks Becker for catching the mistakes I didn't even know I'd made—and for laughing in all the right places.

I am grateful to Glynis for guiding me through lump-sum IRA rollovers after all my layoffs and recommending stocks that actually worked—proof that good advice can sometimes pay off literally.

I am grateful to Jenny and Patrick Payne and Kandi and Shannon Spangler, for opening their homes to me when I first moved to Colorado. Your generosity made a major life transition far less dramatic than it had every right to be.

Thanks to my damework—a posse of instructors and coaches, practitioners and therapists, artists and athletes—for your guidance, inspiration, and for listening.

Special thanks to Scott, the love of my life, for listening, reading, and listening even more; for getting me out of my "old man corner" and into the fresh air; for his patience when I was skiing, cycling, hiking, shivering, bonking, or otherwise struggling; and for his kindness, generosity, and steadfast support when I was ill, wounded, or simply glued to the *Great British Baking Show*.

And, of course, thank you to all the dogs—past, present, and borrowed—who remind me every day what joy, loyalty, and simply being look like.